the form of our uncertainty

Look

into my eyes.

The same gradual fire

replacing

has its trace in the music

which consumes

all that I am stone

persisting neglicence.

We

take the form

of our uncertainty.

A shared vitality

unspent

eye that startles:

I find it ever open.

— Gil Ott

from "The Children" in *The Yellow Floor*

the form of
our uncertainty

a tribute to Gil Ott

chax press

handwritten press

tucson

buffalo

2001

Some of the work in this volume has appeared elsewhere: Ron Silliman's "Blue" from *The Alphabet.* Mark Wallace's "Magic Words" from *The Washington Review.*

Editor: Kristen Gallagher

Editorial Assistance: Charles Alexander, Louis Cabri, Alan Filreis, Gil Ott, Hannah Sassman, Joshua Schuster, Kerry Sherin, Heather Starr.

Book Cover & Design: Charles Alexander, Chax Press

ISBN 0-925904-32-5

Printed in USA by Cushing-Malloy, Inc. of Ann Arbor, Michigan

Table of Contents

New Works by Gil Ott

Poems

Prose

Responses

INTRODUCTION

Presence

Kristen Gallagher

Ammiel Alcalay says Gil Ott has an "ability to resonate and transpose or apply his own political and aesthetic knowledge and intuitions to other situations…to translate perceptions into politically motivated activities."* Perhaps this ability relates to Gil's self-professed interest in "street level intellectualism," his balance of well-informed polyphony with what Hank Lazer says is his ability to make political "petition" which is "less and less recognizable as rhetoric."

Evidence of Gil Ott's proficiencies have been left in spray paint and street-corner soliloquies, as well as in his work of editing and publishing the poetry and prose of writers practicing diverse tactics and politics. One thing has concerned him consistently: "the struggle to articulate."

Ott believes political action is better worked out in social relationships, rather than solely in the material manipulation of language. He has not been so concerned with making his presence known, as in being present in places and languages, as people and circumstances occur around him. You don't often hear Gil talk about himself: he never promotes himself, has never become beholden to a poetry movement and is not the least bit concerned with heroics. He has made beautiful things happen by his willingness to "be a part of nothing," to "be the poem." He has accumulated a humble wisdom from living as an artist and activist, a wisdom he has by all accounts brought to everything he's done.

Ott realizes educational potential and uses his knowledge to great effect in arenas of protest, in articles and editorials on arts and education, and in dedicating years of work to the "Poetry in the Schools" program, educating children through Philadelphia's Painted Bride Arts Center. Crossing genres and politics in ways few can manage, preferring to undermine existing ideology without substituting new dogma, a defining poetics for Gil Ott is elusive. His tendency toward self-interruption and uncertainty, his sense of temporality and the tempo-rary, make him something of a trickster, or as Andrew Levy refers to him,

      dear trouble maker

His acceptance of uncertainty and his history of stirring things up in status-quo-ville are the defining qualities of Gil Ott's poetics. As Chris Stroffolino points out, Ott "challenges some of the guiding assumptions of the political and social efficacy of contemporary avant-garde poetry." One thing Gil says he has often reacted against is the assumption that "people seek out order," claiming he has "always felt the need to maintain a certain independence." As he says, "for me, a lot of contextualization is actually decontextualization."

Perhaps much of Gil's work gets its distinctive edge from his ability to hold tensions and attune to complex, often contradictory senses. His most recent book, *The Whole Note,* manages both lyric and lyric's disruption, both nature and society. Earlier works such as *within range* and *Traffic* maintain tensions between prose and poetry, between immersion in the moment and reflective explanation. In all of Gil's work one can find a certain pleasure he refers to as "the satisfaction of articulation" — a presence of hearing and saying, of finding relation through more relation.

Government was therefore an attitude (Ron Silliman)

Gil Ott governs by observing and maintaining uncertainty in the integrated act of living his life. Kerry Sherin asks Gil about the "political or ethical motivations behind uncertainty." It seems to me that Gil has a radically democratic, detective-like intelligence which keeps him tuned in, attentive, on a path which is intuitive, musical, and which comprises ecstasy, loss, and new beginnings.

Through recently developed endeavors, such as the Philadelphia Publishing Project, Ott continues to locate new and fresh voices committed to writing, artistic autonomy, and community. He continues to innovate and surprise in his own poetry (for instance his new phonetic works which appeared in Combo 4) and to support new projects in his own and the next generation.

Gil, for all you have done, and continue to do, this is but a sliver of what we would give back.

*All quotations in this introduction are taken from pieces contained in this book. Unattributed quotes are Gil's.

Publications by Gil Ott

A Time Line

BOOKS

2001: *Traffic (Complete)*, Chax Press, Tucson, AZ. Poetry.

1997: *The Whole Note*, Zasterle Press, Tenerife, Canary Islands, Spain. Poetry.

1992: *wheel*, Chax Press, Tucson, AZ. Poetry and original prints.

1989: *Public Domain*, Potes & Poets, Elmwood, CT. Poetry and essays.

1987: *The Yellow Floor*, Sun & Moon Press, Los Angeles, CA. Poetry.

1986: *within range*, Burning Deck Press, Providence, RI. Poetry.

1985: *For the Salamander*, Slash & Burn Press, Philadelphia, PA. Poetry.

1985: *Traffic (Books I & II)*, Singing Horse Press, Philadelphia, PA. Poetry.

1983: Single-artist issue of *Origin* magazine, Kyoto, Japan. Poetry.

1983: *Ladder*, Spectacular Diseases Press, Petersborough, Canbridgeshire, England. Poetry.

1981: *the children*, Tamarisk Press, Philadelphia, PA. Poetry.

1979: *Maize*, Pentagram Press, Markesan, WI. Poetry.

ESSAYS

1997: "Holding the Door Open: Gil Ott Interviews Homer Jackson,"
> *High Performance*, Vol. 19, no. 3.

1995: "Sharing the Future: The Arts and Community Development,"
> *High Performance*, Vol. 17, no. 4.

"The Village of Arts and Humanitites," *High Performance*, Vol. 17, no. 4.

1994: "Art in Context: Industrial Pittsburgh Catching Up with Bill Strickland,"
> *High Performance*, Vol. 17, no. 3.

"The Arts are More than the Avenue," *Philadelphia Inquirer*, Editorial page, 2/3/94.

1992: "Community Based," *Short Subjects: Newsletter of the Greater Philadelphia Cultural Alliance*, Vol. 17, no. 9.

1990: "Work to be Done," *M\E\A\N\I\N\G*, no. 7.

(untitled essay), *Tyounyi*, nos. 6/7.

"Art in the Neighborhoods is of and for the People,"
> *Philadelphia Inquirer*, Editorial page, 1/16/90.

"Popular Education in Philadelphia," *Cultural Democracy: Journal of the Alliance for Cultural Democracy*, no. 37.

1989: "Far Africa," Review of *When My Brothers Come Home: Poems from Central and Southern Africa* and *Nightwatcher, Nightsong*, both by Frank Mkalawile Chipasula, Central Park, no. 15.

1987: "Managua Letter," *American Poetry Review*, Vol. 16, no. 6

1984: "Language is Human Community," Interview with Cid Corman, *Paper Air*, Vol. 3, no. 2.

1980: Interview with Jackson Mac Low, *Paper Air*, Vol. 2, no. 3.

1979: Interview with John Taggart, with Toby Olson, *Paper Air*, Vol. 2, no. 1

1978: "Formal Prospects," review of *Between Silence and Light: Spirit in the Architecture of Louis Kahn*, *Paper Air*, Vol. 2, no. 2.

1977: "Hiroshima Now," *Paper Air*, Vol. 1, no. 2

sketch of Gil Ott, by Gerry Givnish

New Works from Gil Ott

Poetry

I am calling forth a poem.

I am calling forth a poem.

Come help me sing the song.

Come be with me the poem.

- from *Public Domain*

Solidarity

"How when I put up my antennae
the world's buzz oer
wells not deep enough
to hold the dead I

back t back off. My
creed's argument, n's claused
fr mete survival — wot
good's a corpse, s's no

r solvent at sick
victim shit, ooze a gut
whine's bord, all flatulent.
Na. Carve it up. Come

pretty pretty progress m
eater limits, my back yard
aroses ground an ear
me out. I i i've gotta

say sun'n hell t boast
a cracker shot, suck, indio
principalis piss — yg
step on a few roaches

d'we (bite) are the world
(chew) homily d spite h big
pichchur n'a sea's sparkly
mirror (swallow) aw (spit) sa

flaw. I tire f certain t't
out. T'ang cod of gadda sod
patch, moan backyard n homo
neurotic wife and kid to high

dense eke a secret life.
Men titled end serve it
's outside the calculation period.
Now. Workin' I due f'you?

Heaven

From the park
to the parting of the waters

one ball of tinfoil
one avocado
three sticks of gum

the small leaves of a fiddle
fern feathering and evenly spaced

t'endure
common inhumanity and neglect
t tier n tier yr

step measuring light a gain
strew holiness strain
sa frosted window
less aperture

'sall around us, the light, ever
she finds everly
dust magnified t'hit n ent her
up here eh among d
d zzl glorious err t terror

atop a tower

swats me, runs up behind
n hits me on
th head w a baseball
flutter determination
walking
smell of rain,
staying in the rain

am
a thing most solid, to myself
counting
foot
falls twenty forty sixty breath um ar
t'beats

b step a break-
fast (toast, jelly, cof
was it Monday, St Peter's,
meal on Tuesday (holds
body and soul
two

dollars tend
r pass n'out t'be

vulnerable, hungry, deprived
of sleep a wking
dream

a' millenial flight, in
the upper air a door
wraith th there y
see! ch born n unborn
waving fore t wrd m
welcome, pulled
up and in co
hearing call — a constant ring
ing heaven's annular core

us among the missing — ha! — a fool
t'take their money, lie

abed thr
shelter how
thll pull y'in m'

arm's s started t'tingle ll
get arrest bray
thing coming shallow w
the weather bet
b better het th
fourth street bridge
early, get
a ledge up

bets a doorway

step pace pr count ten
leven thirteen four phase sun

light sharp to clouded sharp
cold to stifling
heat, winds cloud's
evanescent passage or the earth'
s a system so bright

I cannot
see myself I am more likely
my shadow

here, in Heaven m
m multiple n no more
use for a name

Note: "HEAVEN" was commissioned by Glenn Holsten of Philadelphia's WHYY TV, as part of the
"Poets and Places" series. The place, in this case, is the Benjamin Franklin bridge, a 20's era suspension
bridge, a baroque celebration of industry and human achievement, incorporating the only means by
which one can walk from Philadelphia to Camden, New Jersey. Performed, "HEAVEN" is monologue, a
composite of several shelter residents who I have known over the years.

On Learning of the Death of a Poet

For Daniel Davidson

What I cannot do to music
and removed, having listened
without hearing, to fail and fail

t'attribute rs t'dying s
remedy deny mine
n y passage so accurately

distor ted or ment, I lack
brtly demonstrated. Ycleave
th flaw b lie b art m

pale neglect, I cannot
soften bread in salt
I lone wndr r, gone.

Child, aye, n stumble up
on awe soliloquy ea diminishes
us. Wr

tng me, all unprepared, n
echo stain, unchanged,
unchanging, laugh it

lost imaginary, could
escape yr interpreter, evade
the harrowing metaphor. G

wch y grant.

Thirst

trip nminute's
digital ghost whips
air in the hollow

hiding her face as she runs, or was
that a fabric moving without

range, every inch
of skin, each muscle and the soft
function

moth
ing room to room undetected
and to myself

nearly strange.
Interrupt n nightly rope a tense immobile
twist prohibited

d light inhabitant craves
fleet gimme checks
s somnolent inhibitor walking
among a self strong and ragged.

Thirst denied, addiction's
ironic pass-a-hand/face
at the glass

to solvents fumes deeply
abandoned. F'ew
look at it morren once

it crumbles, it teases, it
chides and punishes

at the shimmering brook, afraid

with bleach and breath's revival
unacquainted
to take a step

conceived, rehearsed, debated,
weighed, disputed,

withheld

against a wall
where there is no

touches myself, and feels
me touching
and decides
there can be no purpose

enjoying bodily
dusted interminable thinking

& spittle.

Skunk

Of detritus
up and counting,
so'm to poetry: midst and apart
my generation.

Ode tavoy
t creatures underground
mix form weaning
the sweet, sweet

apoplect g chance semantic
account. Rhyme
me out. Flew
days catched

behind me, breathing
hard. Bits
of plan swarm
short of relic:

my behavior isn't noticed.
What fun! Look
how they mate!
World to tickertape

round the big
bend, atoms exhaled.
Three, for the most part,
words per line

sums a stanza
's premium p form
a ask Alice
I think she'll

clam on memory.
Consider
the shape of the back of the
head, its ascent

through candle flame,
and while you're
aroused a prick
to juice it

up your autobiography.
This, this poem perhaps, this
is your first
hand to stroke

a thorough, sensual
grip a little woman bound.
Shit. Git
all over the rug

n titer pussles
average pone. Where's the out
a dream a child a lull

in a bush arms
promised? When yr
dead the cells
g'on gunk

a skunk's first
philosophical muse.
Chells lk chells splattered
n spread abt

the floor shiny
dotted mercury, a mess
a gesture cdn't
get amidst.

The cheese stands alone.

The farmer the the naked and scarred
acquisitive hook resists the insinuation

of the word that planted sprouts a myth
that threshed and tied a net to trap him, grunts.

Heigh! Ho! The bankers pinch the pink,
Old Man, on your Wife's cheek and scuff

your seed up two per cent, up two per cent
the soil that you also owe somebody, groans.

Time out! Time out! The pinwheel skull
the hot hot fizz of silver silver phosphor

where your eyes go haywire takes
the dog takes the cat down a windmill's

pretty patch and steeple, see the people
out to lynch a commie or a Jew. Are you

the derry-oh, the fink, the snitch, the one
betrayed the bitch, the child, the cow, her dowry

of cheese?

Poem, for Willa

Were it told, my
maple-girl, my paper-warm
October girl, the beach
ahead of us would speak our name as one, a sound
that only ancient water churning
ancient gravel utters

with authority. Our storied
origin in seed and metaphor
perplexes yet, and yet demands
the question and its tensions be
relinquished, love, how

chrysanthemums purple, mantises
their foam and futures know to make.

sketch of Gil Ott, by Gerry Givnish

New Works from Gil Ott

Prose

Evidence

Because I am vulnerable when I sleep, I bundle and tie the evidence with a heavy string and hang it inside the chimney from the flue. Without my leg, I can't get around like I used to, but when I do, it's often up the chimney passage I go. This version of freedom is easiest to manage, fronting as it does directly on cold, starry night. I've been too trusting, and too often cheated in my life. When I was young I indulged in the common fantasy of free will. I traveled, and adapted my trade to local opportunity. In one town I was a cook, in a larger city I delivered the mail, and so on. In a small town in Puget a fisherman let me live on his boat while I helped him winter in, paint and repair, mend nets, getting by. I had a tiny wood burner to keep me warm, and nights bundled in a sleeping bag I'd stare at those orange coals and rock with the water. The water is huge, heavy and indifferent. When the fisherman's daughter came to see me one night, and then began to visit regularly, I never asked her mind. Her body was stocky and familiar, like an armchair, a convenience. The skin covering her squarish face was taut, though not necessarily young, and, despite her general lack of expression, intricately etched. I could see she was troubled, but I did not have the patience. I left that place without a word to anyone. Everyone, I have learned, keeps secrets in plain view, and we all, by some unspoken contract and fearing our own exposure, agree to overlook. Perhaps you think this sounds utopian. You have no imagination. When I talk about my experiences under water, you call them fiction. Your reliance on entertainment is debilitating. Do you find my desperation diverting? When I describe that first moment of panic, having entered the water and then feeling the weight pushing down on my shoulders, what do you call that pale little twinge that you feel in your gut? And since you don't believe in your own experiences, you can't accept the calm which comes over me when I stop resisting and finally inhale.

So it is for your sake that I began collecting the photographs and letters, testimony, bruises, documented lies and half-truths, clippings, paraphernalia and talismans that are my evidence. Here is a letter, two, three, another, a bundle of letters from my attorneys, first from Simon Walt, who, I now see, led me on during that first critical year following the accident and surgery, and then from Brian Karp, who continues to represent me, even though he has done little to advance my case. He loves to say to me: "An addiction is an addiction. You find a way out, or you don't. No half solutions." Here are some fragments of teeth. A recurring dream. The doorway is dark, like a highway rushing toward me in the rain. I've waited here before. There's no getting used to the broken rowhouses on this street, or even the one light at the window two houses up, always on. I wait with an increasing anxiety which, with each visit, overcomes my sense of strangeness. Here are two nails. Hold them in the palm of your hand forever.

Catching the light, an amulet, a silver death's head, a pact made over a bottle of cheap wine. A feeling lasts a very short time. After that, you can never be yourself. I will not say his name betrayed me. I have proof of it, here. The light comes down the West Virginia foothills like a messenger of God where we don't need any god. Kick back. Prepare a rustic camp with our machines at the heart. Freed of women have a tough and silent agreement. Cut the ground by swastika, bite, chew, out of my delirium. Cut the evidence the sun is setting. Here is a crutch. I've made shelter on the side of a hill, from a blue plastic tarp thrown over a motorcycle, boots for a pillow. Now it's difficult to cross the room. A chair is in the way, a tile is loose, the water is boiling for instant soup. There are more types of pain than tenderness. Or rather, pain is the tenderness once shown me by a man. He took my incapacity for his own. Try to forget out of need that he is a man, or that I am one. He lifted my right leg and placed it over the left, then turned the two together so that I gently rolled onto my back. He looked at my face, and he brushed the dirt from it. He straightened my shoulders, then, returning to the damaged leg lifted it again and bent it to my chest, pushing and flexing, reintroducing the flow of blood. Share strength, impart confidence, take them away. Here is evidence of my thirst. An x-ray. An ache at every joint.

Why are you still here? You force me to grit my teeth, get up and show you the door. Why can't you simply find it yourself? You must realize that you are on your own. How are arrangements made, for travel, lodging, companionship, in a foreign country, in an unknown language? You pretend to know things you don't know. It's the surface of things that's exotic. Decay is mundane. The sidewalks are narrow, there's a milk-colored stink running in the gutter. Get closer still. Heat and thirst. Sharp sunlight shatters off in several directions, but not in all, driven and inhibited by the sound of unrestrained engines. You crawl through the marketplace believing that commerce will somehow sustain you, and you are confronted by the corpse of a crow. Returning to your room, you sense that someone has gone through your things. But I would rather talk about myself. I am the one who has violated your privacy. Here are thirteen views of the city, all from the air. What looks like concrete and glass is actually a flow, a flower, a surge of dying that sparkles and pushes at its banks. The flood rushes out over the clay plain and where it touches a new palm begins. The flesh of it is unseasoned. It is sensitive to the least touch. Here is the book that tells of it. It is the book of my body. There is no other book.

The Pigeon

She keeps her hands in her lap just below the edge of the desk, according to some constraint adopted when the habit was newer, but now forgotten, as the nervousness at the bottom of it all takes over. Anyone sitting across from her could see. Atop her crossed legs, her crossed hands, the right over the left, all defense. The middle finger of the right begins, itself crossing over and exploring with its tip the cuticle of its next-door index. Finding something interesting, a tiny rough spot, she discretely raises the hand to her mouth, and with controlled pressure pushes that spot into the narrow opening she's made between superior and inferior incisors, and bites. That gets the teeth working, grinding up the morsel, while her hand returns to rest, and her thumb, a concerned but complicit nurse, rushes over to massage the wound. The rubbing, though forceful, cannot be hard enough. The morsel is chewed up too quickly. Very soon the thumb itself is chosen. Following tallman's perfunctory swipe over an existing hangnail, the opposing digit is pushed hard between the front teeth, which clamp down, and, with the thumb's furthest joint against a bicuspid for a lever, her whole right hand stiffens and twists out from the wrist, like a small salute. This is a more successful tear, freeing a gradual, but unmistakable drop of blood.

So it goes. The thumb must be sucked a bit to stanch the blood, which eases the tension some, but soon she's at work on tallman himself, her accomplice and source of intelligence, who is apparently not exempt from the universal punishment.

I don't mean to draw out the anxiety. I've always found her body language fascinating. It's edgy and vulnerable. I'm a little sorry it's come to this. Surely that's why I'm taking so long looking over her files. Not at all kind, with her sitting there. She knows what's up, and I've read over everything here more than once. Frequent tardiness, here it is, documented. Not very focused, I guess. Can't seem to meet deadlines, and often needs to go back once something's done, to repair it. Just not a very good worker, but that's hard to quantify. I haven't quite got the language down yet. Maybe that's why I'm taking so long.

My eyes on the files on the desk in front of me. Hers, too, though in a gaze. The sound of her stockings rubbing together, as she recrosses her legs.

Or my own hand on my inner thigh. I should remove it, let it stay there a moment. The drowsy swell. Between the incipient speaker and the spoken to, a child in polymorphous glee. Standing over the fallen girl, even as the teacher strides up. Irrelevant brute, a grown woman, I could not have seen her coming up behind me, though I anticipated her angry hand on my shoulder, turning me around. My defense is no defense, my gaze unfocused, my fingernail between my teeth as she scolds me. The pleasure of release, of hitting the girl who'd teased me, of knocking her down. Biting down. An atmosphere all bickering, all children tense in spreading conflict and me the focus, relieved with a punch. The flock suddenly lifts, startled. Chewing. The little shred of cuticle flesh resisting deliciously. All in an instant attending the harsher blow of words, of punishment.

But any word can be a seed. You've got to defy words of consequence, the ones that mean to take your life from your control. Subject them to the doubt all language scuttles under. They will resist; they will twist in you.

They. The two of them. Man and woman. They worked on me for weeks, gathering the courage to cast me out. Mine was the unstable utterance, all potential outside known relation, the third that came invited, then stayed too long. Talk and talk, I would talk toward some undefined climax, but never express love, or even attraction. Sam and Lila wanted, finally, the words to do their proper job, to define a distance, to expel me. This is not their problem. They are, at the beginning and end, man and woman, suspended in the risk that hides in the next fold or crevice of skin. They have determined their ease. Imagine her moving slowly with her tongue down the dividing line of hair on his belly; he leaning back, his finger curious at the folds of her vagina. Their eyes are open; their eyes are closed. They are complete. But none of us had known their intentions. How much of them arrived with their groans and squeals, down the bare hallway to the door they'd given me, next to theirs? How else were they to invite me in?

This child came into their lives a bit too soon. I came as an adolescent: all misdirected, useless beauty. I did not speak the language. My desires were absolute and contradictory. My attraction to the woman was a pure brook, to the man a swelling wave. It was all flattery to them. Not enough to divide, nor to cement them. Mine is a speech limited by speech itself. A speech that fails in the equation of power and lust. A scrap of torn cloth, the rubbing together of stockings, a vulnerable glance, the shredded, dispossessed erotic. They cannot be held. They must be seized, torn out, and forced to submit. A man is civilized only so far as he accepts this fact. A boy comes too quickly to violence. Or watches it occur. A boy cub has no power.

Poor baby blue, all pouched and pampered by his ma, took drowsy to the blue, the blue hill side, the berries there to find. And blue, poor baby blue, the blue, blue berries in the every hot sun did pick and pick, his mama by. He ate his fill, until, until his head did fill, and buzz, the buzzing bee did glide, and down he lay, his mom preoccupied. A cloud did pass. And pass alike a mama bear, her baby bear, to likewise pick, and eat, and stumble on, the afternoon so lazy by. So lazy bear babe wandered off her mama bear yet unaware, the field so blue, so sweet and warm, her baby gone. The other side in shade a sleeping baby blue, and little bear did wander there, and lie. Fair clouds continued passing by, till mamas two at once in panic cried, they cried, their children absent in the wreath of vetch, and out of sight. Their simulta-neous cries did fetch, not kids, but eyes, a pair of eyes in fear, distrusted species nigh. A cloud stood frozen in the sky. Blue animus unfurled, prepared to fight, defend, to die. That frozen cloud came softening, as children two at once came stumbling, stumbling from a shady lea, and parting for their mothers two did turn a moment, facing each to each, good bye.

Some whimsy in my head at times confronts a messenger, confutes a message clearly given. I'm not listening. Bud and George stifling a laugh as I enter the elevator, Mark ignoring my greeting at the coffee station. Squeezed into clothing that's too sharp and too confining, their words forced out in little belches of instinct. All the brilliant thinking, all the hard work, go begging without instinct. You get a reputation. I'm the one who watches, sees nothing, and in return for being allowed to watch, forgoes respect. Give me a dirty job to do. Keep me out of the loop. Keep it secret. George, for instance, I'm sure has slept with one of the secretaries. Who couldn't see that? And what does she think about it? And what do I? And what am I to do when the boys gang up and go hunting? I work here, after all. Give me a gun. Sacrifice is the name of the game. I've got to make a living.

Keep up appearances. Learn the language. My own tongue is a woman. She is a playmate, a squealer, and a liar. Not to be believed. A child can't distinguish between a fiction and a lie. But I'm not a child. Even my own words, expressing my own frustrations, seem theatrical to me. This is power. I can do this. For the first time, I notice the length of her stocking, her thigh exposed beneath a short skirt, above her nervous hands. I cannot help but look at them. They are beautiful.

A typical scene: It's a quiet morning on Croskey Street. One by one the rowhouses open up. Mothers, fathers, going off to work, the older kids to school. Here comes a father, bursting out the front door and through the tiny yard, growling in play like a bear, carrying his young boy, kicking and screaming, also playful, under his arm. At the gate, he sets him down, "Got t'go t'work! You protect mommy." He leaves, striding up the sidewalk, and the boy dawdles a moment in the front yard. His attention is caught by a spasm in a clump of grass near the neighbor's wall. It's the pigeon. He'd forgotten about it. He thought it would be dead by now. Last night, before his daddy came home, he'd broken its legs with a trowel. Then he'd held it tight, inexplicably sad at the loss of a friend. He'd meant to care for it. Now he couldn't touch it, didn't want to look at it. They carry disease, his mom had said. He took a piece of burlap that was sitting there, and put it over the bird. Then he went inside.

Academy

Love. My love is small as a bat. Perhaps a bit larger: a winged flap folding over on itself. A black handkerchief. An admission.

Unfold the flap it is starry and black. It is limitless. The opening to that place advances and contracts. A few drops, clear and precious, enter there and become fixed. Love leads me to understand that this is not a place, and it is gone.

I hold my love secret against the others, yet it is a secret commonly held. We turn out each morning, a yeasty aggregate, hungry. Having slept several to a bed, each longs for another out of reach, concocting a self which pushes and bruises, suppressing the discovery each thinks is his alone.

Who has the authority to catch and tell, and who to set the rules? Billy was caught needling in the closet. He was a wee wee. He ruddy all down the hall, in front of us all, Master Hastings following fiercely. I can say I don't. That's easy and true. Yet I do.

We wake up each morning over coffee and the acrid smell of new leather. This being the busy season, the tanning process goes all day and night. Each boy gets one hard roll: plain, cheese, or lingonberry. For this we are expected to work all morning, right up to the first class. After that, there are meat sandwiches and beer, followed by more studies, and athletics.

My favorite is soccer, a free form brand for which we make our own rules. The body is the purest poetry. All of us dressed in silk, in a line, our arms twined and many of us near big enough to show little breasts. This supple march proceeds toward its goal. Perhaps it gets a little rough; that only adds to the effect. When I am in the line, my hips pushed next to Jason's, or Malik's, the full bulk of the moment penetrates me, and I am lost to the team.

Even after the sun has gone and the cold air sets in, the excitement remains and seeks the little slit between our thighs. Were we without supervision, we would play into the night, but Mr. Banda calls us in for showers. There, exposed before the others, I feel ashamed.

I feel despondent. It is as if I had lost someone dear to me. Why, when the night, which is just arrived to envelop each of us singly, calls my name, do I hold back? She who would know me thoroughly, and who would doubtless reveal a cavity commensurate with mine in imperfection, stands impassive now, back lit, just outside a screen door in an early autumn evening. It's an image I can't shake. I scrub my anus. I linger even after the others have left the shower. I want to cry.

"She" departed years ago. She was an essence I have missed and overcome. Still, if I take time and contemplate, I can see her naked, rising out of the still lake. Her eyes look directly at me. Her breasts and stomach are slick with water. I am the water sinking into her thatch and running between her thighs.

Freedom is just outside the academy grounds. I am complete in myself, and, although my leaving may be awkward and surreptitious, leave. I find, after all, that the academy has no guard, no fence or boundary. The wood at the frontier is actually thin and easily traversed. Only the encroaching cold meets me, my insufficient clothing.

Any road I find will do, leading to all other roads. I hitchhike. The cars are small and fast, the drivers younger and with no more destination than I. I choose who I will talk to. These drivers' faces frost, each succeeding each increasingly unworthy of trust. Pick at the edge of ice up like a scab, the set snarl of a kid at the wheel brandishing a demand for sex, a story, aimless.

The cold lets me preserve myself waiting for better circumstances. Exposure must be pursued gradually, yet evenly. What are the borders of the self? Moment by moment, they have to include all past and future, my eventual partner and offspring, my sure death and afterlife. These stalk me continually.

A moving interior, small capsule of light in the night, may be an unlikely place to meet that future in the form of another young man, yet it is there I meet Willow at the Edge of the Water. Like me, he is dislodged and vulnerable, and feels he will soon die. We are both at the mercy of movement. His skin is coarse, his reach wide enough to seem like shelter. He takes my name, and I listen to his every word. He closes my eyes with the tips of his fingers. He is gone.

In his place is a child running into my arms. Is this my little boy? I grow older as I raise him up and gather him close to me. He resists; I know what I must do. I reach up along his leg, along the seam I've seen that runs there, and find the handle of the zipper tucked beside his scrotum. He squeals wildly, and I am frightened, yet I pull, and the seam opens.

None can explain the violence of daily human relations. My boy looks at me with hatred and resignation, his face shriveling. When I drop him on the ground at my feet, another leg appears from the wound in his thigh. I step back. That leg is broken, with bone visible beneath gray flesh. More of the man inside emerges.

I turn and run. In my dream, the woods are lush in mid-spring. They are my external self. Sometime to come, I will return here seeking clues in the decay of hair and flesh that were to have been my mates. I will seek them in the minute crosshatch of twigs and rotting grass in my little clearing. There, near the house of my Master, I will drink, too much for my little head and task. I will be a boor, and make unwelcome advances toward those I seek in memory. Outcast, I will come to doubt the very honesty that will have taken me to that turn.

But I am speaking in the present. I am awake and it is winter, so I will level with you. There are moments, say when I am walking alone at night on a rural road, my bootsteps crunching without weight in the new snow, that I am relieved of myself. My constant meditation, that I am a seed struggling toward the aurora, lapses. Then I am joined, multiple, frozen and aware of all things moving swiftly about and without me. Then I am without sex, or rather, my sex is determined, and I am wed.

My wife and I have an agreement. It waits like arsenic on the pantry shelf. Take it from the dark and shake it.

Pinwheel

I am tired, having walked such a long way uphill, but even my fatigue is light, like a white jacket which comes easily off and falls behind me. Over that wooded rise a rising medallion, jeweled song of every color, and at each door a girl. Some are red, some blue, some yellow — iron, steel and brass. If I move toward any one of them she is naked, bowing at the waist and inviting me in. I choose instead to lie back here on the grass as the pinwheel spins over me. Reach into the picture and pull it close. Feel my strength. Even as I pull the little girls from their hiding places, even as I crush them against my chest, there are more, offering themselves. They are squealing, each squeal a red smear on a perfect blue sky. So beautiful. Everyone is watching. They cheer as I squeeze the spinning thing, and squeeze it, squirting up like a tornado, the girls' sounding like a moan inside. Then going black.

I come down in the back of Luddy's car, flat on my back with the silhouettes of oak branches flipping by down upside against a deep sky. It seems cooler, darker, so we must be getting close to Temper's place up in the hills. I'm a little stiff, hurt in my right shoulder and ribs. Can't say how long I was out. Jane and Luddy up front look straight ahead saying nothing.

I groan a little to let them know I'm awake. Jane makes a little sideways look at Luddy; Luddy grips the wheel tighter and adjusts himself in his seat. I see his jaw muscle move. Nothing more. Strange how nobody's talking, especially Jane. She was my old lady before Luddy, and we're still good friends. Luddy goes 60, 65, even on these winding old roads, up and up.

I sit back, try to remember the dream, play it over. I like that. Mostly I remember the colors, yellow, gold, and red, like polished brass spinning disks you could walk into. Smooth and ripe as cantaloupe, but metal, a liquid metal singing in my arms and thighs. Funny how on PCP such a good feeling is really the same as a terrible feeling, the ache all over fear like the car might drive right into the side of the hill, right into the rock and underground. Like Jane and Luddy might want to do me in.

Finally we get to Temper's place; I know it 'cause of the sound of gravel under the wheels. I pull myself up between the two front seats and notice Jane's hand wrapped in a towel. She sees me looking at it so we don't say anything about it. We pull up to the cabin and Jane gets right out and walks, a little stiff, it seems, but quick, holding that hand, straight up to the cabin. Luddy kind of waits around.

I'm still kind of dazed, things coming back to me slow. That hurt in my side must be worse than I thought since I have to catch my breath once just getting out of the back seat, then a sharp pain standing up. I hold on to the side of the car, with Luddy there just pretending not to see me. I count four other cars there in the driveway, none I recognize, and nobody around. Must all be inside. Didn't know Temper was having a party.

I feel Luddy's eyes on me all the way across the drive and up the front porch steps. Door's open.

Mostly people just standing and sitting around there in the smoke, some talking, but most stop when I walk in. Big guys, mostly, some I recognize, like Temper, Al, Mankie, most I don't, all looking at me. A radio all by itself in another room. It's dark in the room, and it takes a few seconds for my eyes to adjust. I probably look like I'm staring, but for a second I think I see something black and squirming in a big bowl they've got there on the floor in the middle of the room. One guy's holding a knife. Then I notice Mankie looking at my hand, and I stare him back, put it behind me, I don't know why. Never liked Mankie. It all makes me uncomfortable, so I just kind of nod and walk into the hallway toward the kitchen. On the way I look at my hand. It's got blood on it, a real smear, on the sleeve, too, real ugly, and it's not mine.

I know Temper's got another room to this place, a big room he keeps a lot of stuff in, and it's got a sink and toilet. Door's off this hallway, just before the kitchen. I can hear Jane's voice, all freaked, and some other woman talking, from the kitchen as I turn the knob and push in.

Room's empty, smells rank, like nothing's moved in here for years. Boxes and what look like cages along the far wall, a stuffed armchair, paneling coming off the near, no lights. The sink as I remember it's beside the one window, which is propped up with a stick and looks out over the driveway. I can feel that pain running down my right side again as I walk toward it.

First thing I notice looking in the mirror over the sink is a big cut on my head over my eye. Look at the thing's enough to make me feel sick, and I lean and grab the sink. Funny I hadn't felt it before. No washcloth here, so I run water into my hands and splash it on my forehead. The cold water feels good, so I do my whole face and neck, then get to work scrubbing the blood off my hand. Won't come out of my sleeve, so I just roll it up. Breeze coming in the window feels good on the cold water. Things are getting a little clearer. I think back to Jane, how she wouldn't look or talk to me.

For a moment, things are pretty peaceful. I'm still at the sink, but looking out the window, past the cars out front to the dust on the leaves of the trees, hearing the little brickle sound from the creek runs beside Temper's. Another fragment of the dream comes back, a smiling girl floating toward me from a shady spot on the side of a hill. Maybe my head's still buzzed, since I'm watching the sunbeams that way and don't hear my name the first time somebody calls it.

"Pete."

It's Jane's voice. "Pete."

I don't even turn to say it to the door, but keep looking out the window. "In here."   I hear the handle turn, the door open. Jane's behind me.

"Pete, you've got to get out of here."

"Why. What's going on?"

"You really don't know, do you."

I don't answer. I'm still looking out the window, at Luddy's car now, seeing the trunk is up and somebody, probably Luddy, bent over pulling on something heavy in there.

"These people don't want you here, Pete."

"What people?   You mean Temper?   Let him tell me himself. And who are these other people?

"That's not what matters. They think you'll bring trouble."

Outside, Luddy's still pulling something out of the trunk, when suddenly I can see part of what it is. Just the tip, the foot end of a sleeping bag over the lip of the trunk, and Luddy leans back in and continues tugging. It's my sleeping bag. I've never seen another one that's bright yellow like mine.

Jane must've seen Luddy, too, and her voice becomes urgent. "Pete, you've got to get away from here!   Now!"

I can feel the hair on my neck standing up. I hear the screen door slam and Temper comes striding down to Luddy's car and pulls Luddy up by the shoulder. Whatever he says I can't make out. They're both yelling at once. Whatever it is, Temper's not buying it, and it looks like he's about to smack Luddy.

Then from behind me, Jane again, "...you've got to...."

I turn around and face her. Her face is all contorted, scared shitless. "Fuck you, Jane!   What the fuck are you trying to do!   That's not mine!"

Her face is red, her eyes puffy with tears. Her mouth is all trembly. She can't answer, only nod. I shouldn't do it, but I suddenly hate the bitch. I swing, hard, and catch her beside the eye.

When she goes down, Jane makes a little scream, loud enough somebody must have heard it in the hallway. Those people will know what's happened. Can't go out that way.

I turn back to the window and start climbing out. My side and arm have gotten stiffer, and the pain sharper, and my landing, real awkward after falling about six feet from the window, hard as hell. The cabin is up on blocks, so I roll under into the shadow to figure my next move. Lying there, my whole arm is throbbing and it's hard to breathe. Lots of running, and the screen door slamming. My dream. The girl reaches me. She's all vapor, like blue powder, but warm, covering my body. Her eyes are yellow, and fuse with mine as she wraps herself around me. She holds me. It's like a little cartoon when I see Temper come out from behind Luddy's car. He's breathing hard, and from under the cabin I can't see Luddy. He shouts something toward the porch, the people on the porch, and then he looks. He looks straight at me.

An Interview with Gil Ott

Kristen Gallagher, Kerry Sherin, and Heather Starr

This interview, originally done in Spring 1998 for WXPN radio, was intended to bring knowledge of Gil's work to the large Philadelphia audience that station reaches.

Kerry Sherin: When Dodie Bellamy and Kevin Killian were here at Writers House last year, they said something about how you had been here, in Philadelphia, for so long and that seemed sort of incredible given that there were other places in the country where you would have found more like-minded souls. For instance, San Francisco. Why did you stay?

Gil Ott: I used to live on the West Coast — and moved back because of illness. My personal history is what has kept me here, not the literary stuff. To tell you the truth I've always felt outside of whatever is going on in Philadelphia. In the 70's and 80's I was much more involved, at the Painted Bride, and different bookstores.

Kristen Gallagher: Why did you feel outside of whatever was going on in Philadelphia?

Gil: My feeling is that people have tended to dismiss my work. I represent a certain stance, a sort-of street level intellectualism that folks are glad to know is here, but it has little relevance to their own work or careers. There has not really been an avant-garde in Philadelphia. Partly because of this lack of publishing. Until recently, the academics have been pretty timid, while most of what we've had at street level has been very oracular. What's characterized Philadelphia poetry is that it's a spoken art; there is certainly nothing wrong with this – it's just the kind of poetry that's here. Whitman's influence, well-realized and poorly, is still here, along with the black oracular poets like James Weldon Johnson and Langston Hughes. Trace that line up through the Beats and you've got the Philadelphia poetry scene of the 70's and 80's. It hasn't been very balanced. What provides balance is academic participation. Until recently, that had always failed. The academics have been at the academy, and have not always participated. With the advent of more creative writing programs and more community-based work, that seems to be changing.

Kristen: Perhaps Bob Perelman has had some influence there.

Kerry: I think there's actually a critical mass. Rachel Blau DuPlessis has had a huge influence. Graduates of Temple's Creative Writing Program are doing things throughout the city. Your books have made me wonder what you consider your immediate literary context.

Gil: To tell you the truth I don't really think about it much anymore. It's become a very personal pursuit for me. Partly because I really think of the term avant-garde as being very general. I'm restless. I'm quickly uncomfortable with the finality of statement and the authority of form. The American avant-garde has become very sophisticated during the past 20-25 years. There's a lot of room to play. It's the closest thing I know to functional anarchy. So it's important to resist tendencies to codify or identify schools or currents within the avant-garde.

Something happened in the 70's and 80's around the avant-garde in poetry, which was the creation of this thing called the "language school," which is this group of younger writers who threw up a banner and seized as much of the territory of the avant-garde as they could. I think it was a conscious program to do so. Now that's been done in a lot of different contexts, a lot of different schools of poetry over the years, it's not a new thing for a group to do this. However, I always felt the need to maintain a certain independence from any school or whatever, realizing that I would never be fully engaged in the language program. So, for me, a lot of contextualization is actually decontextualization. I don't know if that's really your question, if you're talking context in terms of a community of writers.

Kerry: Do you think that the fact that you wanted to maintain a certain independence has affected how well your work is known?

Gil: There are other things that have to do with it. I am not as productive as, say, a Bob Perelman. I am not a theorist. I don't write criticism. I'm not a professor. I'm not engaged in the academic community, which would bring a lot of opportunities for reading, speaking, publishing. I don't have those resources. I'm also not presently very active in the more performance-oriented scene, like I was at Bacchanal in the 80's. That's okay. Again, I think every writer needs to realize that at base it's their personal satisfaction that they're aiming for, that motivates them, at the moment of composition. That is what I seek out.

Kristen: Personal satisfaction … with your writing? Being satisfied with your work or your ideas being present in the work? Feeling you have communicated something?

Gil: The satisfaction of articulation. For me, part of that process has been pushing away the cobwebs of alternate forms of satisfaction. There's always the temptation — I'll sit down and I'll write three lines and say, this is going to be a book-length poem, and its going to be a big splash, it's going to be really big, blah, blah, blah, and I'm going to send it to so-and-so. And I've got three lines on the page. That's like one of those cobwebs to get away – because the fourth line is yet to be written.

Kristen: So being more present or conscious in the doing of the work itself?

Gil: Exactly.

Kerry: Which are the books in which you think you were the most present?

Gil: The most cohesive book is *The Whole Note*. I had a fellowship; I had time and a studio to simply do this writing. I could conceive of it as one large piece. Every day I worked on a page. I really was able to develop more.

Heather Starr: Can you tell us a little bit about how you constructed *The Whole Note* and what the different segments indicate for you? It's broken up into four parts . . .

Gil: I'd start with my understanding of Zukofsky. The whole notion of this as a musical form. The structure itself was intended to mirror a whole note, broken into four beats, each of those beats broken into eight partial beats.

Heather: How does the way that you broke up one note into four beats elongate time? You've written this whole book that takes place in the moment of one beat.

Gil: Oh. Well, I guess in retrospect it does. Don't take the metaphor too seriously. It took longer than one beat. [Laughs.] Although I guess if you really got down to dissecting a note, you would have these movements within a note. You know, anticipation leading to some sort of fulfillment. So the sections would resonate that way. If you're talking about time in the poem, you'd have to look more at overlap. Overlap between pages and overlap between sections. What I was predominantly thinking about was social being as coming into conflict with natural being. I was living in a very rural place, and I was observing hawks sweeping down and eating mice – a very brutal but beautiful environment. And I was trying to square that with the notion of "primitive" social beings as they were reflected in ritual. At the same time I was doing a lot of reading about voodoo, which has always just been a fascination. What do I really know about these subjects? I've never been to Haiti. I'm not a voodoo practitioner. It's all kind of an artificial construction. But it becomes a platform for me to explore some more relevant philosophy and to square observations of the environment around me.

Heather: In your poem "The Children" from *The Yellow Floor* you say "we take the form of our uncertainty." What uncertainties are you trying to reflect in different forms? Like in *The Whole Note.*

Gil: That uncertainty is reflected in *The Whole Note* in the little paragraphs which go on for a few sentences and then stop. There's an abruption. That's the uncertainty. It's like, wait a second, I lost the thread, or, wait a second, is that really true, what I'm saying? And then resume. How do you make the leap across that gap? That's what your mind is doing, of course, when you're listening to it.

Heather: Well, your mind is constantly trying to create something linear from those gaps. Part of what I really like about *The Whole Note* is that after reading five or ten pages of it, I had to relax that attempt. I couldn't sustain the effort to construct precise meaning.

Gil: [Laughs.]

Kristen: I think the book engages the faculties in a way that is close to listening to music —
yet the musicality doesn't ease one into any kind of blithe lyrical euphony. It's a broken lyric.

Kerry: Like you said, you were thinking about the social body and the natural body. There's
this dirt under your feet while you're talking, and some desire to speak or sing. It's like in the
opening of *Public Domain* when you say, "come be with me and make the poem." In the final
section of *The Whole Note,* I feel the abruption, but I sense there's also a building momentum
towards "I have stood here." I don't mean to make too much of it.

Gil: No, make it. [Laughs.] "I will make a body of utterance that fooled me." That's the way I
feel about the poems. I have built this body of poems over the years. And then you ask me
about the context, as if it represents me, and I feel like it doesn't, somehow it doesn't. And
the uncertainty — you're very right to pull that line out, "we take the form of our uncer-
tainty." That really goes to the core of what I've been doing.

Kerry: Can we talk a little bit about the political or ethical motivation behind uncertainty in
Public Domain? You say, "The regimentation of meaning is criminal, even in the least incre-
ment" which is on page three. And, "Language is at once ambiguous and persuasive enough
to offer itself as a tool to advantage and oppression and seen as medium, neutral.... Complicity
in this crime as auditor, actor, as much as speaker, contributes heartily to our public behavior
as consumers, workers, citizens. The poems in *Public Domain* are antipathic to such complic-
ity." How is your poetry manipulating, dealing with or responding to the manipulation of
language? Where does uncertainty fit into not being complicit? Is there a relationship?

Gil: *Public Domain* is as far out as I'd gone with something, for lack of better terms, you would
call political poetry. It's a very fine line. Something political always attaches itself to some
dogma, and in that sense always betrays itself, betrays some exclusionary motivation. The fine
line is to write a poetry that wakes people up, but doesn't tell people how to be, or present
what's "right".

Kristen: You would prefer to undermine an ideology without replacing it with another ideology.

Gil: Exactly. Exactly. I mean, who needs that?

Kerry: But how do you escape that?

Gil: Language is common property. We're surrounded by people constantly using it to
manipulate us. It's almost silly to try, as a poet, to find some way to avoid that. I was thinking
as I came over here that I haven't really stopped with the notion of a political poetry. What I
have maintained is — well — if you're doing something that has that goal, of presenting some

kind of critique or making people think in those ways — the most honest way to go about it is to do it on the most basic level of language itself, to break language up in a way that makes people question the order itself.

There's a poem I wrote recently called "Solidarity." I wrote that specifically for a magazine in Pittsburgh called *HEART*, Human Equity Through Art, which has an overt "political" orientation. They solicited a poem from me. I sent it to them and they were offended. They sent it back saying, "We really try hard to publish work that people understand."

Kerry: What are these people not seeing about contemporary culture?

Gil: People seek out order. They want an orderly world. And language is one of the principle things we have that orders the world. Poetry, even among artists and those sensitized to the disruption of convention, is a rarified cultural field. Too often, those who are even willing to go there are motivated by a desire to have their beliefs reconfirmed. It's a rare reader indeed who is willing to have the very technology that anchors his or her beliefs — language — challenged. A poem like "Solidarity" means to get to the anger, the confusion, the uncertainty we feel when we are deprived of the calming journalistic and scholarly rhetoric we usually rely on to validate our beliefs.

Kristen: And we're back to *The Whole Note* again — that idea Heather mentions of elongating one note, one moment, to expose all the abruptions we censor. Stretch some beautiful lyrical moment out over time and you'll see jaggedness.

Gil: That's what I've always done with writing. I'm dissatisfied with an inherited order. Partly because it doesn't work. Your mind is always making the whole out of parts. Even when it's advertising copy or a cereal box. So much of language is built on references to things that may be familiar to you in the world. But accepting it as that alone doesn't leave room for creative thought, or change. It's essentially a tool of maintaining order. From President Clinton on down, everything that he might say is intended to keep us all in line, keep us on track.

Kerry: Perhaps some readers don't want to acknowledge that there's a different kind of meaning in a poetry of this sort. There's a whole different order of meaning.

Gil: Meaning is always constructed. It can be shared — but it's not inherent in the words.

Kristen: The way we're talking about abruption and noise and music, the way interruption and chance reduce intention in *The Whole Note* — this sounds like Cage — yet you are very different...

Gil: There's a real difference. Cage is the ultimate literalist. He's always reminding us that the primary thing is to listen, to receive. It's religious. Me, I'm more interested in interpretation and the permutations of the work through relation.

Kerry: You've talked about feeling suspicious of any group or community. It feels to me as if you have an idea of another way that things could be. I'm just wondering — what exactly are the things that really piss you off? And what effect do you think disrupting language would have?

Gil: I'm a child of the 60's, and I've maintained the luxury of rebellion through alienation. I mean, as far as I'm concerned, everything needs to change.

Kristen: The broken lyric is that, too — rebellion through alienation — unities and breakages can be both alienating and touching. Perhaps poetry is less able to instigate change, but more able to communicate or even embody change. I mean, whether any difference is acknowledged at the moment of anyone's noticing that difference or not — difference, stability, connection and change are always occurring.

Gil: Unfortunately we live in a time when stability is an ideal, and people are very afraid of change. We are told that things aren't changing, and that's just unfortunate, because things will, and do.

Heather: You end *Traffic*, Book II with the sentence, "He is divided and becomes himself." How do you see both your poetry and its relation to your life changing over time, throughout the different things you have written? There seems to be a fluidity between your idea of your self and your writing.

Gil: For me the pleasure has always been in creating something new. I look back at my own development, and it's gone through a lot of different phases. That's an interesting line — "He is divided." But one way of looking at that image is a cell dividing, and that's development.

Kristen: This sounds like your writing process. You've implied that you kind of go with it, let a piece of writing develop as you write it. Can you describe your writing process?

Gil: I got to admit I'm not very disciplined about writing. I can't say that I set out on a project. Somebody asked Gertrude Stein, "How do I become a writer?" and she said, "Write. Just keep writing." Keep it in a file, and eventually you'll have enough to do something. And that's kind of the way it works with me. I can't say that I set out on a project. Someone like Ron Silliman, now there's a project guy. But that's not me. He sets out to write *The Alphabet* and now it's 800 pages long! This poem I read, "Solidarity", there are a half-dozen, maybe a dozen poems like that that could cohere, could become a book. But I never set out to create the kind of book of these kinds of poems. Books, when they occur, mark a period of time.

Recently my writing process has undergone a bifurcation. Since *Public Domain* I've started writing narratives. What that's done is it's freed me up to be more experimental, to go even further out with poetry. They've split out into two very different positions. More performative, sound poems really.

Kerry: Are the narratives you've recently been writing also experimental?

Gil: Yeah, when they work they are. When *Public Domain* was published I realized that to a great extent the poems are narratives which I wrote and which are self-censored, which I chopped up and wouldn't permit to see the page as narratives. I really wanted to be doing narratives. So I challenged myself to write narratives. With prose you start out with a whole different set of conventions — the coherence of sentence structure, paragraph, character, etc. I like the challenge; it's something new and fresh for me. Yet I find, perhaps naturally, that my prose writing can be heavily influenced by my poetry.

Kerry: Where does the self-censorship come from?

Gil: Inhibition. [*Laughs.*] To be honest, it's like, what if someone finds my notebook and there's this ridiculous thing in here?!

Kristen: That line that Heather quoted — "He is divided, and becomes himself." The piece, "Academy", has a sense of a self meeting parts of itself in writing, as if one person contains different characters. This seems to have a relationship to how you talked about your writing process — that you let things emerge, as opposed to pre-planning. Do you believe it is the case that bits of self, when one engages closely with one's language, can get blown up or brought out by the experiment? Or that these bits of self and language end up in dialogue with each other?

Gil: That's an interesting question. Whether they are technically narrative or not, when I began some years ago writing these kinds of pieces, I also became aware of encountering myself in the writing in a new way, which is just another factor. That had always been there. The content of the poetry has always been very personal for me. But I didn't want to be writing autobiography. When you start accepting and working with the conventions of any form of writing, then you also immediately encounter conventions of meaning at the same time.

Kristen: It doesn't strike me primarily as autobiographical. But pieces of some self, or of the idea of a self, spill out. And the writing has a structure that seems developmental, developing as you write and find things and just go with it.

Gil: Exactly. In writing something like this, I start writing and move through it. I don't have a plan, or a map, from start to finish. So the writing does go places that are unfamiliar, or to places I have thought or fantasized about.

Kristen: Places people are afraid to go.

Heather: Or actively avoid. You've acknowledged that setting out to avoid a certain subject doesn't mean it won't come up of its own accord.

Kerry: Why not autobiography? What's the trouble with autobiography?

Gil: There is no trouble. It's sort of a cliché to say that any writing is autobiographical. At the same time, the direct conscious attempt to represent oneself comes with a lot of baggage. The therapeutic side of it, the daunting nature of the task: if you've ever tried, you realize you can't really get it right. The objectification of one's self is the real problem. I don't want to surrender that interpretive moment for myself or for the reader. I want you to listen to this and think about yourself or someone you know or somehow relate it to your own experience, make your own meaning out of it — I don't want you to read it and think, oh that's who Gil is.

Kerry: In *Within Range*, there are pieces of a narrative. It also feels to me like it's somewhat about sexuality, and gender, and the making of one's gender. "Academy" feels potentially incendiary. We're living in a world where here, between us, we might say the subject matter is organic and we can relate to it, but bisexuality and multi-polar sexuality is something we don't really talk about. When sexuality becomes a part of the work, it often doesn't get discussed.

Gil: We're a sexually repressed society. Is that an understatement?

Kristen: Well, there's some outcome to sexual repression that makes one who writes about it need to problematize it. The aspects of sexuality that one might spend a lot of energy trying to cover up — confusions, fears, judgements — that problematizes anyone's talking about it in this culture. There are reactions, repercussions, automatic shut-downs. If you really want to get someone to think — a suggestive, an ambiguity that lingers — that's what might get underneath.

Gil: There are such taboos around people's transgender experiences, experiences that people have in puberty or adolescence, you're scolded so severely for them that you repress them, you don't deal with them. A work like "Academy" is a little can opener. Undoubtedly it's bizarre enough that you can distance yourself, but it's also familiar. If it does that, I guess it's successful.

Kerry: The distance is important, then. If there weren't a distance, it would be dismissable as "that guy's sexuality". You're trying to get into someone's own material, and tweak enough things to say, we're in here together. You can't tell the difference between you, the reader, and the narrator of the story. At least that's the effect it has on me. Which doesn't mean I'm about to say that I, too, had that experience in the shower.

Kristen: This to me brings up a question. In *Traffic* and *Within Range*, you have these sub-poetry texts. I kept thinking subtext. What is operative there? What is the relation between the line-break writing and the text-wrap writing beneath it on each page?

Gil: I wanted the bottom parts to be more prose-y. I wanted to emphasize the difference, the polarities of the forms. The parts at the top are generally direct observations. I used to do an exercise where I would just observe. To get to a point where the poetic language would be that natural. A Zen moment of articulation — that's an ideal for me. Observation is one very powerful way of building poems. But obviously, they are still built things. The other parts of each text appropriate the form of commentary in much the same way.

Kristen: I kept thinking subtext. There's something going on, to point to, beneath the poetry.

Gil: It's interesting — the prose tends to take on — and I call it prose, it's as close to prose as I get — it takes on a more authoritative tone. I can play with that. How much do I want to continue the interpretative moment? That's the play of my poems.

Responses

Ammiel Alcalay

A little history

for Gil Ott

I first came across Gil Ott through early issues of *Paper Air,* shown to me in the mid 1970's by a dear and recently departed friend, the sculptor and musician Brad Graves. Brad had himself worked in collaboration on material that Gil published, with John Taggart. Some years earlier, I had been a reader of MAPS, and even sent John a query of some kind. *Maps,* like *Paper Air* and the dozens of other little magazines that had been passed on to me (*Black Mountain, Origin, Evergreen, Big Table, Kulchur, Yugen, Floating Bear, Neon, Set,* etc.), or that I came to follow (*Caterpillar, Bezoar, Vortex, Fire Exit, Intransit, Intrepid, Io, Living Hand, Text, Sun & Moon, Vital Statistics, Big Sky, Angel Hair,* and so many others), formed a kind of autobiography of associa-tion out of which I might someday be able to reconstruct some sense of myself then. I was living in New York, working at a variety of jobs (construction, building superintendent, auto mechanic/body repair, truck driver, laundromat manager, bookstore manager), and writing. Formally, I took classes with Toby Olson and Gil Sorrentino at the New School before going — off and on — to City College. Through Toby Olson, Gil's presence again manifested itself and, even though we still hadn't met, *Paper Air* clearly entered my inventory of things to look for and pay attention to.

In 1989, I returned from 5 years in Jerusalem, the second leg of a circuitous journey that both greatly 'expanded' my horizons and 'complicated' my relationship to what I had once intuited and grasped — like someone drowning grabs at a rope — as a 'purely' American idiom, as 'the pure products of America' themselves, of which I both was and was not one. I brought with me the manuscipt of what would become *After Jews and Arabs: Remaking Levantine Culture,* a book destined to make the rounds with publishers for four years since it was correctly perceived as a threat to the status quo by the gatekeepers in the field. While my varied political involvements in Jerusalem informed every sentence of that book, the form it took — at least on the surface — did not quite match the intensity that I felt needed to be conveyed about my experiences. As I underwent the natural waves of erosion and sedimen-tation in the process of resettling in a place that had once been home, it became clear to me that I would have to act very quickly to store some messages up in some bottles, before they simply broke down into irretrievable fragments. I began work on *Understanding Revolution,* a piece that in fairly short shrift evolved into *the cairo notebooks,* a text for which, in many ways, *After Jews and Arabs* serves as an elaborate set of footnotes. Naturally, I started looking around to see what kinds of things people were doing, or not doing, and where such things were either published or not published. Several purportedly progressive journals — both politically and formally — rejected *Understanding Revolution,* ostensibly on 'stylistic' grounds. And it was precisely at that point that I remade the connection to Gil, one that I am not sure we had ever actually made outside of my awareness of who he was and the kind of work he was committed to.

When I called Gil to try and reconstruct some sort of chronology of our getting to know each other for this piece, we found it difficult to pinpoint whether we had actually met prior to *Understanding Revolution* or not. All that, however, is quite beside the point. In Gil I immediately sensed an interlocutor who had clearly chosen to undertake a way of life that embodied both his aesthetic and political intentions. As we worked together in editing my piece, I found that Gil knew precisely what he didn't know about the particulars of a situation that I was describing — at the same time, he knew exactly what conclusions the addition of that missing information would lead to. The sources on the Middle East that he was familiar with — literary and political — were just right, and allowed him to build on a solid foundation rather than, as is most often the case in this area, be forced to pull apart misconceptions and false assumptions. This ability to resonate and transpose or apply his own political and aesthetic knowledge and intuitions to other situations was a source of continual sustenance for me, particularly as I felt more and more isolated in an everyday existence whose instigating sources I had to rediscover for myself, in an effort to translate perceptions into politically motivated activities. Here, again, Gil served as an example of someone simply going about his business in a realm of imperfections that he would rather not contribute to by reproducing its hierarchical structures.

In an article on the Lebanese writer Etel Adnan, I have written about the sense of permission that her work gave me to explore a certain sense of historical burden uncommon in American discourse. Not that the burden isn't there — it's just that traces of it have been cemented over. Gil's suggestion and offer that he publish *the cairo notebooks* with Singing Horse Press was another instance of permission, like that of Etel Adnan or the deeper resonance of Robert Duncan's music that I had absorbed much farther back, 'as if it were a scene made up by the mind, / that is not mine but is a made place.' In Gil's case, the place was very made, and very concrete, and we worked out the details together, slowly and with great care, from the photographs to the size of the book and its odd reverse order, in which the lines of each fragment end at the bottom of the page only to scroll back above or below the horizon line represented by the elegantly side-barred numbers a third of the way up each leaf.

It is this aspect of Gil's work and presence (and I use the word deliberately), that I feel most in need of emphasizing, that is, his role as an editor and publisher, particularly in this time of small and large scale conglomeration and wholesale carelessness. Within *Paper Air,* Gil managed meetings between covers that would have been difficult, if not impossible, to achieve in 'real' time. I find Gil's ability to move across aesthetic and political lines in a local, unpatronizing, non-ideological and generous way, still all too rare. At the same time, he has managed to remain fiercely independent and completely uncompromising — it is out of such fabric that the best of our culture, a culture that we can claim to be a part of, is woven. As such phenomena become recognized more generally (through, for example, such magnificent documentation as that represented by Rodney Phillips and Steven Clay's *A Secret Location on the Lower East Side*), Gil's past and present efforts with *Paper Air*, Singing Horse Press and The Painted Bride, will find their rightful place in American literary and intellectual history. It is indeed a distinct pleasure to be able to, even in such a modest way, publicly recognize and thank Gil Ott for the essential work he has done and continues to do.

Charles Alexander

Two from Cardinal

7/11/00

(Gil Ott)

flying Tatlin's glider

or a paper horse

       through singing air

into the public domain

      where moon

      (it does not run

      on gasoline)

filled with whole notation

finds where history

        has left us

(it has left us)

        or is there dissent

        in the stone, where

        the book imposes

        incalculable requirements

as if air as if song

      and a space between one

      group of words and another

to lie down among

7/11/00

(Gil Ott, Julia Blumenreich, Willa Ott)

jewels glow and breathe out

as though stars go somewhere

                  else

headlands to desert to

streets with stone houses

all in all, black ink white paper

rubbed or printed

        where the lines

        bear or redeem

little but the organ's intent

to form a language

of us, our homes are yours as will

                  as well

it composes, blooms whether little

or much water recommends face

to face

        wash over the children

        in the light

        before it goes

Bruce Andrews

G O

— (a mapping / to & fro Gil Ott)

[Politics as Explanation, Politics as Prescription] —— what must be done —— [Praxis nests on understanding, resists the know-nothings] —— A primer little more than no explanation. —— [But words' reach can be explanatory. And we can tease prescriptions out of them] — — Steps prescribed, resistance turns a minor note the gathered // in animal defense —— Doubt to surer politics, braking downhill.

A 1. TRANSCENDENCE

[Idealisms don't work as politics. The vanities of transcendence — as a premise, or as destination — start to seem like a phobic reaction (to materiality), a big-scope skepticism (as dematerializing), the rejection of closure reconfigured as the embrace of indeterminism.] — — makes no sound —— The regimentation of meaning is criminal, even in the least incre-ment —— oppose // iconophraty to determination —— [Construction would put 'on suspension,' so would everything non-natural:] —— the putting / together of parts, artifice —— [But downgrading these, or inattention to these, risks escapism.] —— utterance / in sensation / duplicates / flight —— past the eternal

A 2. REPRESENTATION

[Transparency, or Translucency: as the basis for representation, for easy access to Image & Identity; pictures & expressiveness.] —— eye that startles —— prudent to the objects —— FIGURES —— audience / always less than one —— [To mirror; to enmirror] —— or the eye cannot confuse —— given ear given access —— Filled by throat. —— smoothly / moving / in and out, / the facsimile, / deeply / felt —— [Representation isn't necessarily static; it can move, it is 'moving,' yet still at risk of Possessive Identitarianism.] —— Control's conceit, out of each substance's specificity gobbled, flickers at the idea. —— violated, by a language making so much fucking sense to me.

A 3. NONREPRESENTATION

[Big Question Marks, Emptyings.] —— culminating the image / no longer engaging —— the insubstantial images —— to opposite image —— as your losses / become opaque —— [Presence, representation, in doubt; or with matte overlays.] —— ceremony / forgotten —— In the negative dream —— Every object blank when I am looking in my mind among injuries.

—— Ignoring the word in me. —— I've got nothing more to say. Dig elsewhere. ——
[Critique as anti-doxa, as liberation?] —— Will to erase will be damaged by orthodoxy. ——
effects / object object believing discarded —— words untutored —— [Dissensus /
Unsensed, Unsensible] —— in the dark / extended

A 4. PROCESS

[In the wake of all this romanticized (enfeebling?) nothingness: a reaction, a micro-materializ-
ing, a micro-content. A miniatured clarity, or presence or gesture —— at work, fragment to
fragment, moment to moment parataxis showcase.] —— a line drawn thinly / to define a
plane / of particular resonance —— [Processural leverage] —— outside our text's necessary
reference. —— The heart mismanages // tactile share. —— materialize... accord with
experience —— in the immediate —— leaping out the condensery! —— gesture's / pure /
means / accumulate / the vertical —— [Or, if not miniatured verticality / content, then:
preoccupation with the 'top note melody' / surface of Process-based formalism.] —— scrape
up art from surfaces unbidden —— metaphor // thin / as // the laboring hands / withdraw. —
— in headlights / or a head throb, doting on minutiae —— Ate my fingertips —— this
precise increment / distances —— That that that. —— [Microprocessor: the New American
Poetry, say, with its underpinning dependence upon Image & Identity. Fragmented self-
conversation, self-talk — as nest.] —— the disorganized proximate / making of me

A 5. MEDIATION

[All of words frames path. Form — a fuller mediation through the body of Language; less
literariness than languageness.] —— Anybody's guess assumed a map of alien terrain ——
Inequivalent in method, but essentially questions —— that place your mind only / accommo-
dates hemorrhage —— whatever is to hand / unravels —— [Gesture disintegrated by wide-
angle (& not so wide-eyed) attention to language, while — by something akin to overall
mediation, maybe even meta-mapping.] —— Let the device destroy us. —— Form as
mimesis — to spin & sweep in circles, or concentrically totalizing.] —— vague potentialities
pass into circular imitation —— [Generalized Abstraction] —— for the word / grants
latitude

B 1. SIGN SYSTEM

[Signification: the rawest of raw material gives us atomic & subatomic opportunity.] ——
Serially fixate —— fragments value —— the less and less form assuming —— of particles /
composing —— Full of paper's bobcat —— [Abstraction is part of it, but now we also have
Unitizing/Nominalizing. Display Grid Adventure: defamiliarizing all by itself, & especially when
set in motion.] —— Raw sensory equivalence an animal tongue —— Ennerved —— cell-
rigid —— what gathering of atoms —— one / of-a-kind / without value —— a model strung

/ binary, unity of resistance / mesh —— a pinprick in a poem —— times / mute spasms.

B 2. SIGN TROUBLE

[Signs are made to be ...] —— breaking the code —— in definite trouble, tie / down those already secure, friend —— [Politics as explanation as breakage] —— quickly cored / to cacophony's / mazes —— One equals a sum of transgressions —— [Discombobulation, Gibberish, Nonsense, Arbitrary organization, Dissolution of Subject.] —— Signifying not at all or everything evades identification —— out

multiplying signs, actual voices out / of synch —— spin convulse —— the subject / liquid / seeping —— Unbalanced to the next // without a subject, belonging elsewhere

B 3. DISCOURSE

A word; nowhere to rest. —— Person unnecessary, address diffuses. I can report to you that he. —— fenced to burn individual meat, acting out me, the author, the pleasure of every company —— [Discourse as language's address to itself — recovering form as something mediated through use. Framing — or rooting, or constellating — even the most extravagant flip-outs of 'raw' material.] —— how plain expression accumulates a code. —— [For writing to navigate within discursive seas, studded by personal handles. Discourse as Dissemination, Osmotic Theatricality. It frames (& empowers?) a less individualized action. It trumps the isolated voice; it trumps Formal Systematicity — we're not just talking langue/parole here.] —— only patterns seem brilliant, and fade. —— I will build a body of utterance, that fooled me. —— But each has his use. Squeam a little here, a little there, soon everyone knows you. And you are abundant, available —— that illusion of form address implies —— An agree-ment we rewrite

B 4. READING SUBJECT

[Readership defines the individual as active appropriation of the collective] —— My daily appetite insults a system. Grace at prey, convective after. —— and I am the body of this moment —— I may not own the language but the meanings are mine. Whose homogeneity? —— equating solitude with labor —— a man as complex / of the between / coherence —— two // as town at once, but from / oneself curiously —— PRIVATE LIFE —— the interior recovered

B 5. DIALOG, AURA

[Absorption, & a static a-social kind of absorption at that, returns as dialog with Language] — — is intransitive implies you. —— magnified parcelling you out teases alterity. —— [Mimesis,

a domesticating mimicry, a copycat trick with mirrors. Not through depiction of persons.] ——
—— in animal defense —— more opaque // to our accord —— [Presence as Opacity, a
bedrock collective impossibility] —— I may lose

consciousness, but society continues. —— [Especially as a language — in which even what
you don't remember is written.] —— dialog, / the plane variously / open —— dances to
reconcile —— are reconciled

C 1. DISTANCE

[Artifice & non-artificial distance — to liquefy, defamiliarize.] —— Moving, variant
ornithography —— in what show fluid —— the self-evident over —— less... than presence,
the transmission... or any other problem set to right —— separated from me / by a device.
Practice —— reliable disintegration —— Contradictions endistance; they create the basis
for authorizing, for sustaining authority.] —— to dominate,

again, to suggest a safe distance —— [Or: to suggest an *unsafe distance*.]

C 2. SOCIAL CONTEXT

Language accretes, and molds itself around the precipitant moments of a culture. —— World
once in a grid spies the natural it out of it filth —— [Smorgasbord] —— turned their
propaganda on themselves —— [As a tourist in my own life....] —— and simultaneously
finite the subject of classification can't rebel. —— [The relentless particularizing process] —
— fill my silhouette —— responsible / surrendered, meek —— tamed irony / counts / pulses
—— by opposition detonated / bodies of men —— habit to gloss —— [Put the gloss back
in glossolalia.] —— have at me, all you want —— Habiting ... inkling who, to whom I'll
receive my utilization. —— body / 's troubles subsumed —— a tense identity violating mere
whereabouts —— [Social context: badge or angle, domesticating or enlivening: 'identity' in a
still only depersonalized, prepackaged version.] —— Questions, toasts, confession, sugges-
tions.... lead. To me. Look at it from my point of view. From consensus hums like a house, or
other pleasant-sounding logic —— The rest of language is out on strike.

C 3. SUTURE & INTERPELLATION

Welcome to this image of yourself, sure as I imagine you. —— He is divided, and becomes
himself. —— all puffed up, a caricature. My disagreeable bifurcation as well —— Able solitary
laws to grow in me If we're figures to ourselves, / what device will free us? / Some play. /
Characters have characters / to trip us up. —— [Role theory] —— heart's a machine ——
identity, mine determined / to undermine a diagram. —— Be be be baby. —— you / recede
and grow numerous.

C 4. APPARATUS

[What's not to like? For example, beyond interpellation, the current shape of a fuller Social Semiosis, Consumption as Reproduction, the Spectacle, Simulacra & Machinic Reterritorializing. No longer are just codes at issue, but an extra layer of materiality: regimes of bodies, code-dissolving spectacle, institutional apparati.] —— Reproduction itself. —— the vehicle, who only a moment ago thought herself a machine. —— Am rhetoric could kill the speaker —— The imperative levels address. —— fuse / an engine's power to your threat / that we / remain divided —— become domesticated corn —— Reduced to a twitch —— It is our smallness / frames criminal use in the world —— [Size — of subject & object —— as complicity, as malleability] —— consumption —— reinstate / distraction —— under capitalism... —— [Beyond the commodity's ability to absorb all opposition is our champion-ing of *interactive* (not microphone-vatic or stroked passive intimist) reading experience: an *informalism* taking shape inside, between, & outside the words.] —— by commerce / the compact given to doubt

C 5. PRAXIS

[Need keeps the book of lying open, the language common to all ——Yet this is a counter-utopia, as if language were only a communal scarcity — with its part/whole relations sparkless] —— Small angelic accomplice / lost to night, fuse —— whole scrabble to douser —— [Yet the particular instances of *weighted freeing* offer something extra, something of a *social mimesis*.] —— My currency in yours, grace. —— out of us shocked a full life. —— [And rematerializings. An encompassing dialog made out of 'social outtakes' — & already socially coded materials, sometimes already commodified into equivalences, currency, atoms — from person to duo.] —— Make / a dance of that. —— night's signs —— trace extremities —— a pace implies home, identity —— wide and wide —— Operative we, the varieties of pace argue and agree —— [An informalism, *une musique informelle*. Carried far enough through through the social (through & through):] —— investing the common, redeemable dream.

Anonymous

GO TILT

come on & crawl home sweet
to me ma & one day you'll
get to grow all mansize
& everyone will avert
their face just in time
to say they did not see
it happen but then they
always thought you might

TO GILT

I am the mistake. I am the horizon beyond which your talent will not take you. I am as well
the solution, the false faith to which you surrender with relief.

A shiny thing, an acoustic flourish, a confession, the self, a future incarnation, an impression, a
promise.

I cannot be retrieved. You must look beneath the surface. You must lose your way. Cover a
failing. A lie becoming true through articulation corrodes the glittery shit.

GOT LIT

That which is alone insufficient, which sniffs about for clues, which claims the whole of
fragments, society of solitude, knowledge of impression, a cloven character advances,
passionate, engaged, and thoroughly dissatisfied, pushes, through forested anxiety, a corpse,
a flowering revolution, scent of clove that stays in the vicinity, a monument of sorts, two or
three girls at random, lightly walking, all around green, to this you wake, you take stock, you
establish yourself, the epithalamium, forward or reverse at once universal in scope and
bound inexorably to the failure of utterance, o girl, by the narrow hips, the indifferent
shoulders grasped, a musky scent, as in any drunkenness, any youth reiterated, as never
once did occur, so the book, its chapter paragraph and sentence, so the implicit
predecession, the desert continually, erased.

Julia Blumenreich

Clear

for Gil

way up until
the red neck
of a maple,
your long limbs
on the sky;
the handle

to the dipper

Gil Ott and Julia Blumenreich

This sequence of thirteen poems was written collaboratively in 1985. Passing the notebook back and forth over a period of weeks, it was a way we came to know each other.

Poem #1

Call on
the pleasure of that small disturbance
no one

two

activate

Poem #2

stone sculptures
carved outside
the transit stop

in relief
"…the deepest station in the city."

looking down, she's dizzy;
and up, the worker's reach

Poem #3

Plant whose
virtues have not
yet been discovered —
one particular,
watching over

the hold on
the home free
the away where

indigenous lessons
pause over
cornflower
sky, the inside of a petal
least of all separate –
how tallness happens

Poem #4

subject to tableau
stands thus, are it contra blue
since the subject's

more the soundtrack. They dance,
we dance. Wind
that will bring rain.

Poem #5

The vane senses
for instance we
were nearly up in

Mercury sweeping the drapes
aside
happened happened happened

first notation: the house shifts

Poem #6

among houses, each

form on leaving the familiar

Poem #7

intervene, two hands to disassemble
enterprise itself. Care and uninstructed

sense to me. My beautiful friend arrives
in sumac, the scent of her parts

to move on one diagram
deprived of commensurate time.

I'm content. Four steps
confound a reel

suggests a window, or fragment
still in the midst you'd see

Poem #8

numeric memory the one,
two, the more and

All is essential
or restrictive, hours'
unadornment aggregates from
there we discern *such*
a tiny every,
underfoot

is planning and is elevating
"voices like golden trumpets"

recall   while they begin,
not a buzz assembles
our misses.   One seize
over another   one hand
over   do onto

Poem #9

reach
along   or is it
your
                              game
                              violates
skin's equilibrium, an eco-
abstract as a third who talks
in phases. One of us
          to myself
          around, reaching

under no
difference

Poem #10

preposition as of description
into words   =   script
          long tresses
          a man's belt wraps
some multi-colored bobbins assuage
a table from a cable spool

latitude (lass) as other's arms
round out length to
perpendicular easy dimensions
R & R (you & I reading &) or
have equal
grow up to trees

a piece of paper lies level
if or — tosses until
stops transferred

Poem #11

As you age, a table
companioned. You on the vertical, I'm flat,
a paper record we
were. What more?

have no advice. She dreams her
blue and yellow dirndl spinning.

Poem #12

theory of differences
don't watch him going to prison

or the wind up her skirt, even
grammar the same. Your inventions

not my waddle though there've been times
at table
we've gone driving.

Two, animal
legs, two hands.
Make work.

Poem #13

Chronologically:
stood still at the edge of the field
was observed, perhaps
then broke
the law
omits passion and cause. Certain
lamentation from a select
you, enough to numb
haste. Couldn't get
out if I tried. The blades
of grass
cut me, damn poetry.

Craig Czury

Walking The Bloody Fifth

the hill
    down
  church slag
into
    bells
  at suppertime
            the mines
gil
    the mine
  cigarsmoke
            what was mind
    smell of cabbage
reaching into
                implodes
        the vein

Rachel Blau DuPlessis

A Note on Gil Ott and Community

Gil Ott has been a moral, intellectual and organizing force in the Philadelphia poetry scene for many years, a person who enabled many of the things we now take for granted — especially a real community in poetics. He is a principled and noble figure. When he began *Paper Air* (in the later 70's), his was the only place in this city that proposed and was curious about significant innovative writing with an eclectic perspective, bringing under one rubric strands of New American Poetries, Black Mountain, Language, procedural, and ethnic work — a little like *Hambone* might be said to do now. Gil's desire to know, to formulate, to understand, his real curiosity and perspicacity led him to create issues about or centering on Cid Corman, John Taggart, Jackson Mac Low, British poetries, and early language-based poetries, as well as sections on translation of Japanese and Spanish. This journal had a significant impact on me, and was one of the places one went to get news and meditation. *Paper Air*'s title is significant — the paper through the air, the air filled with paper airmailed back and forth, the arc of intensity, scrupulous and honest interconnections created: "first conceived of as a newspaper for an imagined community of poets" (as he says in 1984, in volume 3, 2). Gil also took the risk of such work — the early issues had a kind of 70's raggedy look, which soon matured into a notable large format magazine, looking like *The Difficulties* or *Avec* would later. The statement he put forth in the second issue sums it up: "not the final product but an accumulating by-product of their correspondence, *Paper Air* momentarily frames the movements of the artists here participating." Correspondence is a key: word-letters between people, and the sense of communion and community built on honoring differences, being eclectic, and examining developments justly. The work is conceived of as a "resource" — a place to grow from, to move with. The magazine went for about ten years.

During those years, the journal took a prescient stand on the political tests (implicit or explicit) that were driving granting agencies, the resistance to "poets engaged in radical linguistic and social analysis." (This in 1979.) Community-based presses and readerships were what Ott proposed. And what he created and supported, in his curatorship for poetry at the Painted Bride. As those of us lucky enough to have been published by Singing Horse Press know, this press is another example of Gil's cultural creativity. It is very definitely a community-based press, but one with a national community. The paradox of the local and particular being the only path to the statement of scope — William Carlos Williams' paradox — animates Singing Horse Press. Its books honor it, as it has produced its books with honesty and care: I would want to single out especially the works of Harryette Mullen and Ammiel Alcalay. I have always loved the look of my *Draft X: Letters* that appeared under Gil's aegis, and the intersecting puns on letters (mine were the qwerty alphabet) and correspondence — that key word.

Gil's poetry wants to plumb mystery — the mystery of being here in survival, and love, and of acting through sprints of language in a swift-eared playfulness. But it also wants to point to the afterimages of political dilemmas: as in "Models topple // unresolved and the road not taken, taken, / stinks." (From *Public Domain*, 12) And Gil himself has been motivated and made more aware in a very difficult way: through the costs of physical pain: "The forgotten // wound may be too great to finish telling. No source to it, the / illness moves." (*Public Domain*, 24) His is a subtle, swiftly shimmering poetry. Gil Ott has been determined, through many years, to return the gaze of the world with firmness and justice, and to bring about corre-spondences among our many communities and the one community: of poetry.

Norman Fischer

For Gil Ott

I remember meeting Gil here in California, at Green Gulch Zen Center, after a Dharma talk I gave one Sunday. I remember I had centered the talk on a poem by Wallace Stevens and Gil seemed thrilled by that: I think thrilled is the word. His face was glowing. To think that this Buddhist stuff, for which I think he has an intuitive feel, was not anti-literary, but could be rather a supplement to, a friend of, even an augmentation of, the art of poetry, that he has spent his life practicing and promoting. After that Gil (he was at the time artist-in-residence at the nearby Headlands Institute) and I went on a lot of walks together in the hills around Green Gulch. We'd walk for hours, talking on and on about what mattered to us both. Love. Family. Honesty. Surviving. And of course poetry. I came to appreciate and look forward to those meetings, and I miss them now. Gil has spent a lifetime dedicated to working in poetry and aiding others in doing so. It hasn't been that easy, I know, and there have been many moments in which giving up seemed attractive, even necessary. But never really possible. As time goes by I see that it is not so hard to be a poet, to write, even to write well, to publish, read, review, and so on. But to sustain that over a lifetime, to make a life of it, and to touch many other lives in the doing of it, with kindness, and in support: that is difficult, and that is what Gil has done. I am not even here mentioning his own work as a poet, which is beautiful, consistently so, and challenging. But his accomplishment, I believe, includes his own work but is much wider than that. As it always is with a poet who is truly important.

The work included here, called "Subject Matter," was commissioned by Gil a few years ago. The proposed project came very much out of the initial impulse that I saw in Gil years before: a desire to explore and affirm the relation between Western poetry, particularly experimentally inclined Western poetry, and Buddhism. Gil asked three writers with significant interests in both fields, myself, Leslie Scalapino, and Alan Davies, to collaborate on a book that would tie together these strands, and would include some expository material about them. The project did not come off: Leslie went on to write a work that is a book in itself, Alan was not able to participate, and I also wrote probably more than would fit into a three way collaboration. The section below is the entirety of part two of my five part work. It was written out of my study of Western post-modern scholarship on the koan literature of Chinese Zen.

two: the subject's self-definition is never analyzable

Nishitani's strategy in zen aporetics

of the koan, loose lipped with ripples

playing about the edges

no girding of forces no lunch and no retreat

so abusive to evoke Harold Bloom's hand

drudge resistance of expression then he would

handle this

the endless shopping and improvements

toward "kenosis" and "metanoia"

breaking toward a radical discontinuity

toward horizon's meaning

the social praxis

like an assembly line (lone

poet contemplating waterfall as flute plays)

of sexy cars in Dearborn

out of the ordinary no doubt according to thought

piled up in fleecy adjustments

of what did I mean by what I have said

or what did you understand by what you have interpreted

or have you configured yourself anew based on what you thought to include in your interpretation which was original

or previously meant in other contexts fuller arguments

as if a text assembled from parts parts of a person

(Sung texts discussing T'ang materials that did not exist previously suspect certainly a loop and a twist to be making

transhistorical or extrahistorical claims while

based on spurious history repeated solemnly with a straight face)

as if a person leached from out of gathered materials

locatable streaming out at you with heavy context

(Kathy Acker dead in Mexico)

flipped through pages and pages of or online

"However the key to the transmission paradigm

was the incorporation of the Confucian sense

of ancestralization including

motifs of succession"

and consciousness itself (to mention the unmentionable

which is not "Western" nor "Eastern," neither modern

nor ancient and yet only appearing in any way on the basis of

expression a particular form of difference

bowing and chanting sitting immobile and so forth

picking up on a particular sense of life isn't all

theory) is an endless series of face to face meetings

in rooms with particular appointments (red rooms)

tangled and tangled vines entangling: what you thought

was confusion turned out to be exactly the ticket

which is to say there's no confusion like confusion

nothing to get rid of all dressed up with

everywhere etc. "here's looking at you, babe"

and anchored in a debate whose terms

flap in a furious wind

deficient in historical accounts

language debunked by pantomime which turns out to

be an even more degraded form of language (a question

rather of how the little girl holds her doll

whether she is going to squeeze it and break it or drop it

or will she set it aside altogether and grow up)

more likely entirely made up

not to be dismissed in a single sitting

sky grows bright and dark by turns all day

radical critique of

"my whole point about this system

is not that it is a misrepresentation

of some Oriental essence — in which I

do not for a moment believe — but that it operates

as representations usually do... representations are

formations, or, as Roland Barthes

has said of all the operations of language,

deformations..."

that the cars do roll off desirable and spanking new

is itself no cause for alarm although it is quite persuasive

the world over

our mode of freedom and exhilaration a basic right

or rite — to roll down the highway with my suitcase in my hand

toward setting or rising sun or moon

mode of conduct or contact

amazingly founded on ancient dead ones made up later

mummified or purported to have existed in the way they did

scarce and being used up entirely even in our youth

and at the same time destroying all in its wake

if you want to look for blame there is plenty of blame

you better look or it will eventually find you

me in the grip of it unable to release

or even notice smell of green grass newly cut

or dry wood heated and smokey with pitch

"misheard the term due to faulty comprehension

of spoken Chinese"

had been quarreling over and the argument unfair

but how make it stick so serious and colorful like a rug

semi-serious so made to be in it by the shape of the language

folding up so much of the history I lived through

cut while shaving and bled

polarization and valorization of zen

strangling terms and limp lingo to be repeated

and repeated with a coercive meaning

how allow the person's tears

time repeats material repeats itself

amazingly founded on ancient dead one made up later

is itself no cause for alarm though it is quite persuasive

is semi-serious so made to be in it by the shape of the language

or of time itself

the same day relived a million times in one time

how allow the person's tears

(hard to say complexity ambiguity contradictoriness)

and the book before we read it already clear

(and less clear after we read it far less clear)

"a text purporting to contain knowledge about something actual

...is not easily dismissed" but what about a text

that contains non-knowledge about nothing or pseudo-knowledge

about something that isn't actual?

"zen.. is particularly clear and adept

in recognizing the need to subvert deliberately

any attachment to or fixation with

the symbol-making process" in other words words

only mean something for the moment but not seriously

which is what words do do as words or groups of words

organized either paratactically or hypotactically

pulled up all at once with a parbuckle and — oops! —

rolled back down again to the bottom

which is why we read it

to hear our own thought echoed back

and I am standing feeling the wind and rain once again

(which does not suggest actual wind or actual rain

and even the word "actual" has nothing to do with

wind or rain it has to do with talking and listening to talk)

more a moral force than just some convincing words

particulars in their astonishments

any abstraction kissed in elocution

the pleasures of thinking — and what isn't thinking

or mediated by blessed with thinking

organized around structures in air

("everything solid melts in air")

known as the person — person's locked

(there he goes saying all that stuff again

that everyone's always saying again

amazingly founded on dead ones made up later

mummified or purported to have existed in the way they did

of spoken Chinese

semi-serious so expected to be folded into the words I used

and that would be the function of words actual words not actual

winds or trees

and in defense of which standards

interior gateways and encumbrances

looks like barriers and critiques

the person's swimming in his eyes up to here

and "koans are a kind of religious expression

that has an element of vagueness and mystery

based on nonconceptualizing nearly all religious symbols

to some extent to cultivate opacity

ambiguity elusiveness and enigma in order to create

an indirect communication

triggering a subjective

realization

of truth" such as it is in this day and age

semi-serious in spoken Chinese scarce

and all but used up even in our youth

but able to bounce back and at the same time

destroying all in its wake

experience not language but language is experience

not just one thing at a time but everything at once

two streams of photons don't pass through

(not suggesting anything can fit not suggesting random parts)

for honestly I've forgotten how to cook

brought the trope to bear finally on the weather

concealed the obvious

which once revealed ceased to be the obvious

and finally set fire to the house

Eli Goldblatt

Defined Anarchy: A Note on the Poems of Gil Ott

I have known Gil Ott for over twenty years, and that long friendship makes this note a difficult one to write. I don't want to embarrass him with personal anecdotes that may do little to gloss the poems, but I don't want to give the impression that, like the perfect New Critical poet, he has led no life outside the writing. His work, in fact, does not lend itself easily either to autobiographical interpretations or traditional exegesis, but I do think it's possible and necessary to say something useful about the poems. I'll spare the reader my anecdotes and say merely that Gil has always seemed to me both strong and vulnerable in ways I admire very much. In his verse those qualities have translated into an ability to follow a demanding and critical poetic and at the same time remain open to his caring and responsive sensibility. He is never a cold poet, even though his work can be at times tough and resistant, and I would like to share with you here a few thoughts about Gil's poetic project as it has grown into a life's work.

Gil's words shift and slip past the reach of the greedy, comprehending mind. I glimpse images and find myself dreaming whole stories when I read his poems, but often I don't discover these phantasms in the lines when I reread them. Yet I know Gil has been there with me, for his art is subtle: "The poem is public event, host to a multitude of private entries, a defined anarchy" (*Public Domain* 3). The "private entries" represent lived experience and momentary surges of feeling, but he resists fusing these entries into a consistent or sustained persona, despite a Whitman-like ambition for the poems: "Look for their author on the street, driving or walking, at work, thoroughly exposed. Look to yourself" (*Public Domain* 3). Thus Gil's work remains warm and emotionally engaged even while his language presses the reader to take her or his own stand inside the poem rather than search for a dramatized self to focus and make sense of the landscape.

His poems are some of the richest lyrics and most trenchant anti-lyrics I know. The more lyrical impulse of the early poems collected in *The Yellow Floor* approach at times the gritty spareness of Williams' "By the road to the contagious hospital." Here are the opening lines of Gil's "Fairhill":

> a bird—of any family,
>
> small and bright—
>
> rises
>
> startled
>
> from a cattail thicket

wide and wide,

the freeway

to the refinery and taking

in a mud-gray creek,

tribes speak

color

the self-evident over

and patient   (2-3)

The bird appears suddenly but isn't identifiable perhaps for the same reason it was startled: the traffic noise suppresses naming, and the hurry of a freeway makes lingering impossible (Williams' Model T over against Gil's little Honda). In a different culture (perhaps an imagined tribal culture), humans might see, name, wait; in this one we can only note fragments, hints of "any family." As the title poem "the yellow floor" suggests, we witness this unfinished and fleeting scene and, in witnessing, gather the traces into lyric: "at departure open / joining / traces / extremities" (9).

The lyric becomes eclipsed in Gil's more polemical but highly-charged *Public Domain.* That book takes up a struggle against contemporary "regimentation of meaning" (3) and refuses complicity with consumer capitalism through a many-voiced and resistant poetry, as in this passage from "Talking around":

In on its complicitous, gnawing inside. Am rhetoric could kill the

speaker, taste of blood like copper. Ate my fingertips. Greed, the

object, 's words untutored from a mouth. Sick. Knocked out a tooth.(7)

The language becomes violent—literally breaking apart—but also put-on, exaggerated. Is he suggesting that this speaker personifies rhetoric ("[I] Am rhetoric") or, more likely, does he conjure up an American public discourse so malignant that it murders even its own speakers? The lyric, the emotional moment in time, appears here, but it is framed and held at bay:

observing any given

through

But I'll embellish what I see, seeing in fact sentiment.

resistance, not as stone, but stone

better left   (47)

the embellishing, nearly threatening, voice warns sentiment away even as the eye perceives through a sort of resistance that is not stone-like but stone.

In other poems Gil reconciles or brings into colloquy the lyric and the anti-lyric. The sustained poem *Traffic*, written in the years just prior to *Public Domain*, allows both impulses to converse across *Traffic's* doubled form — verse above and prose notation below — any one impulse flickering back and forth from bottom to top. A later work, *The Whole Note*, successfully integrates the two impulses in a sequence of poems that balance the "private entries" of lyric with more public pronouncements.

> Bark and fennel stalk destroyed, scattered
>
> scent winding in the same field the violent
>
> macadam, wires and traps. Monotone and
>
> irrational acts listen this bag of ribs is letting
>
> wind! By hurry
>
> mean debacle at hand. Transform in habits a
>
> colony, tests his vocal cords, cries out at the
>
> people who invented him. In every case the
>
> imperative case
>
> too to wait for rain and be a part of nothing.
>
> Muscle in the skin pull to a gait presence,
>
> even
>
> surface and interior. Night is more familiar,
>
> run ordered there. Lacking breath, redirect
>
> wit.   (second page of section 2/4)

Here I see an encounter with a stick-like cantankerous old man, someone almost out of the Spoon River Anthology but also as large as Williams' city / man in *Paterson*. I smell the fennel and the fart, but language also whirls about, warning that words we use will shape any encounter and spoken commands ("imperative case") will "redirect wit" even as it must "be a part of nothing."

Gil's recent short stories, unpublished except for three brief pieces in *TO* #5 (Summer 1995), prove that he can shape a narrative which is not "linguistic ornament" (*Public Domain* 2) and yet partake in the on-goingness of traditional fiction:

> But, as I have said, a tunnel is a passage. I have not wasted my time in
> waiting, but have examined this place thoroughly. Since its beginning, it has
> begun to show signs of its illness. Large polyps the size of breadfruit hang
> from its interior walls. The walls themselves secrete a sticky fluid which
> collects in puddles. These are very difficult to avoid as I crawl in the
> darkness toward the awakening I know will come. (40)

Though he sketches characters and action in few words, the stories come over as surprisingly substantial and intriguing, half-Kafka and half-Japanese ghost tale.

Let me conclude with a single memory. I remember visiting Gil years ago in Blue Bell, Pennsylvania, where he was staying with his parents just after his first successful kidney transplant. We sat in his bedroom, a room like a necromancer's den piled high with books, in that well-kept suburban house otherwise innocent of verse. Later we walked in the woods behind the house. Snow had recently fallen, and Gil couldn't walk very fast or far. The path was circular, and we walked around and around talking about Emily Dickinson and how a young man like Gil could not easily write of the death that had come so close to him. From that day to this he remains one of the strongest men I know. He's strong and vulnerable at once, and that is the hallmark of his music.

Karen Kelley

Diptych for Gil

the lines don't say that, and can't be made
to — the calm precision of human testing
can help him. Or not.

1/4 = motivated by loss
2/4 = myself on suggestive nights
3/4 = it does seem
4/4 = the you in question

especially towards the end, a
kind of love

alone

your back. Needs the book of nothing in the lines after all

I have made a
mistake. The voice remains, as before, jolted by uncertainty:

   I will body the odor
and I
will nevertheless.

//by definition unstable: there is no way
to measure

The fact of the "bottom" may indicate the physical world
and not really:
a. reluctance
b. others have their insistences
c. this is also a form
d. as a position
   (that is, an ideal,
   but others have their insistences

and do not think of duration)
makes it unclear whether a "form of
one walks again and again" even as it slips away from us,
that makes the funhouse because it lets
us experience
//visibility: hidden
//position: absolute.

explicitly
fragments of the foolproof circuit

Red Chair rising from behind observations
like: *provocative hand, please me*

a pattern,
scribbling, lettering and the isolation
against an empty ground (single blue wing)
equally beautiful not for contrast but for resonance.

The imprints are also perplexing.

others have a slightly blurred quality
linked by a cord
or wear a child's cloak
and you are very sad

And the man tells you there isn't any emotion
But you do not understand the words
often hung in groups on festive occasions

and in the present those blacked out captions
(horizontally suspended guests)
through wing-clipping and disparate internal scale
resemble stones, drops of water, corpuscles.

The edges on one side grow thicker,
a humming Frigidaire, Venus of Willendorf

"wet into wet"
holes and desires
not diminished in size nor detail lost

along each rib
arrowline finials, some ochre and some peachlike

the fillings have different strengths:
spermatozoa, agates, flowers and fruit swerve into one another.
Often there is one big swerve being peeled or folded back,
pushed toward the center,
hardened cake icing,
corps etranger,
realm of meaning and concern.

Seven of the ten layers consist of the line between statement and question,
notions of the actual interrogated by repetition.

Demo:
#layer1 which is an avalanche of glass fragments 120 by 228 by 253 inches
#layer2 as if appearance is a sheet folded in half resulting in four pages.
#layer3 the "shot" is the fundamental unit in the flux of the world, the selection itself
         constituting submission.
#layer4 Complete with pictures
#layer5 brings him to the halfway mark
#layer6 This kind of ambiguity of scale
         residual & verbal: 1 & 1
         possible / clasped
         a bowl and I tap it with a spoon like a curious vertigo-
#layer7 Ink to the breathless force or
         a very few notable exceptions:
         in hand, drawings and graphs, photos, a 6 column page and a headline more
         than one column wide

         a question upon
         the cumulative ongoing
         no less opaque to you than to me

         PRECISELY

Kevin Killian

On Gil Ott's *The Whole Note*

I went over the summer to the Marin Headlands, to act as a judge on a panel—determined to get my young friend David Buuck his residency there. A big panel not only writers but visual artists, filmmakers, performance artists and "sound people." All of us to argue among ourselves about who was the best and most deserving and talented of the applicants. This was the site where much of Gil Ott's *The Whole Note* (Zasterle Press) got written. Three-fourths of it in fact, and the last part completed back home in Philadelphia. Part of the National Park Service, the Headlands Center for the Arts exists as a handful of large weather-beaten white houses strewn across the frightening hillsides above the San Francisco Bay, and artists are given residencies there year-round. Some meals included. Stand on tiptoes you can see the Golden Gate Bridge gleaming red and snaky through the fog. The ocean's way down there, somewhere at the ends of the footpaths that lead to the beach on every side of each inlet. Cautiously, one hot afternoon, I picked my own way downhill, nodded at a few tourists who'd come to photograph themselves against the familiar skyline of the city. "His own neighbor," Ott wrote, "to appear himself uplifted, and elsewhere, victim of the theft erodes way of going under." My feet stumbled and fell, in their familiar city shoes that were meant for pavement, not this—what was it? These paths hidden by dried beach grass, flattened berries. "I meet him on an isolated corner, we exchange punctuation to intelligible adjustment, through his eyes." These are the steps, I told myself, down which Gil Ott passed, the staves of *The Whole Note* composing themselves in his head as he, too, must have stumbled. I shared his vertigo at a remove: I'm a city boy too. I'm not good at this Ansel Adams stuff. And my head wasn't filled with poetry, no, with tactics, how was I going to get my candidate past a panel of ninnies? "Compare paranoia," Ott wrote, "twice old bird out of hell to ruminate alone." I didn't see any old birds, just a flock of inexpressively young starlings lit up at my feet and whistled away high into a field of gray and blue — this huge sky that put me on my mettle, ruminating alone. No birds out of hell. These birds came from some unusual place that must have been egg-like at the beginning, and how startled they must have been, when the eggs cracked and they found themselves at the Headlands. For it is a place that seems simultaneously brand new — raw and aching — and older than Time — thanks, I suppose, to the ancient waves that roll up and down on the beach in perpetuity. "Up and express my will his habits contemn my knowledge of his failing exposed." Terribly weary, but that's the fate of us Californians who've come so far we can't really remember Philadelphia. We have come to the land of the Lotos Eaters where it's hard to get any work done, except screenplays, of course, or Lou Harrison-type gamelan symphonies. You look at a bird — the bird looks at you, its yellow eyes soulless in the waning sun — and within what seems minutes it's only a delicately articulated set of bones. "In his ease those listening as well, a board stick jammed where bone had been, the crown of a tooth spat blood, or rum, collapsing, then standing again." Well, there were bones all around me. Tiny bones of birds. That's what happens once you turn 45 and you don't look carefully where you're going. But someone listening? Humph. This was like a poem by Jack Spicer where the ocean's roaring on and on in this eternal melting drone of birth, death and driftwood. Or that Shakespeare one where those were whatever that were his eyes. "The steps, once lost, are never exhausted." I wanted to do the thing he, Gil Ott, did; to come away with a profound experience of nature — or of human intervention of nature — example: those proud military houses standing bolt upright after so many years of holding their own on the slopes of Marin. "The youthful look a drug deserts wants in, that is, out with me, from here."

It's not that we're not the same person, I reflected later, reading *The Whole Note* again, but we don't have the same name. There was something country, or at any rate Hesiod, about his name, Gil Ott: not pastoral exactly, but bucolic: "gill, an organ for obtaining oxygen from water . . . To the gills: as full as possible." Beneath it a siltwash of other associations: gila, I thought, gilt. The sun, glancing down at these grand hills, that had once washed California almost to its knees, into the sea, saw me for a minute, but then looked away, as though passing someone on the street you slept with once and it hadn't been pleasant. "Gila," I thought, "gilt." If this seacoast was "majesty," then let me out, send me back East to the tottering little houses and stones. The slow, sonorous build-up of the Marin portions of *The Whole Note* catch this panic in suspense; Ott doesn't mind the rising tide of contradiction, since its analogue is in music. In the way that a whole note builds up to a bell-like richness you don't get here. "That was embedded in his name," I replied to myself. And what about how "Ott" reeked of "otter," the Western animal with feet completely webbed and with claws, the ears small, and the whiskers very bristly—

Was he in a Beatrix Potter book?

—or some Ernest Thompson Seton he-man, he-boy book I had read as a child long ago back East. "—and that have dark brown fur highly valued for its beauty and durability and when dressed resembling beaver"?

This is the passage where the sea lions swim in and out and congregate in the rocks below the Cliff House, lying in the sun, rubbery gray skin perhaps quite hairy and matted close up, but shiny in the distance. If you wrote three parts of a great book here and then went back home to Philadelphia and finished it up, it would have a progression of music: not that I understand music. Only highs and lows. "Ottava, at an octave higher than written if placed above the staff (ottava alta) or lower than written if placed below the staff (ottava bassa)." But maybe this was just in my imagination as I shrugged, pulled my windbreaker closer around me, and made my way to the reconstructed Army barracks to force the vote my way. The birds are gone, the bones gone, all the way up I know only vertigo in the colorless empty sky.

Hank Lazer

Inquiry Notes: Gil Ott's *The Whole Note*

> Need keeps the book of dying
>
> open,
>
> the language common after all.

0 / 4

I don't know Gil Ott. I write this first because reading is, in part, a complex way of knowing (or of getting to know). In most essays, we don't discuss how we arrive at a reading of a particular text. In this essay, I hope to make manifest a phenomenology of reading, which may include passages of stumbling toward a productive relationship to the reading/writing event and a gradual sharpening of my reading and writing. I hope to pay attention to *how* we get to what we read, including odd, curious, coincidental social connections. An essay usually presents a carefully selected and edited lyricism of reading (by erasing processes of arrival). I have in mind an essay that might become a demonstration and embodiment of reading-as-attunement that seeks a generative dialog *with* Gil Ott's *The Whole Note* (Zasterle Press, 1996).

I pick up this latest book by Gil, and I begin to think not so much about the text itself, but about our changing modes of connectedness. I have corresponded a bit with Gil, and nearly ten years ago I wrote about his book *Public Domain* ("Technician of the Social: Gil Ott's *Public Domain*," *Black Warrior Review* 18 [Fall/Winter 1991]: 106-116). Over the years, Gil's press, Singing Horse, has been a source for some tremendously important poetry for me, especially Harryette Mullen's *Muse & Drudge*. We have friends in common; I've heard wonderful stories from Ron Silliman about Gil. *The Whole Note* includes a note locating the writing of the first three-fourths of the book in Sausalito—not far from where I grew up, and a location for a current poet-friend-correspondent of mine, Norman Fischer. Recently, I've e-mailed back and forth a few times with Mañuel Brito, publisher of Zasterle Press, and Mañuel and I have swapped books.

Books do not fall out of the sky. They too are part and parcel of our networks of friendship, of a shared passion for poetry.

Gil's new book bears with it the mixture of democratic invitation and complex investigation that I think of as fundamental to his poetry.

As I enter this book, its markings keep me mindful of musical notations—the section markings 1/4, 2/4, 3/4, 4/4 also being musical measures. The first two sentences of Gil's book

> **Our sea, to rough trade cautiously ap-**
>
> proached. Pea green and troughing, sounds
>
> **like poetry.**

make me mindful of sounds as a pathway through the work, **rough** and **troughing** being key. The layout itself alerts me to varying possibilities of what goes with what and of how poems may be measured and set forth on the page:

> **Our sea, to rough trade cautiously ap-**
>
> proached. Pea green and troughing, sounds
>
> like poetry. There's a license finds me
>
> at wild anise, out this window facing one of
>
> all the hills to the sea run. Prominent stalk to
>
> yellow promise, ordered and notified. Able
>
> solitary laws to grow in me
>
> excrescent, damned, never enough. Exterior
>
> **to year's own narrative, one's evolving mis-**
>
> calculated hunger, or hunger's tumor. Weed
>
> be beautiful, be beauty, dependent
>
> simply in anticipation of youth drummed
>
> everywhere but home. Take and use. Dis-
>
> criminate. As in laying,
>
> scrape up art from surfaces unbidden. My
>
> **body standing next, compared to what a wild**
>
> seed produced. I walk away.

Stanzas? Sentences? Lines? Are the stanza breaks indications of new beginnings? What modes of continuity and discontinuity are being suggested?

License. Anise. Promise. The premise of one perhaps subliminal (musical) path. A sounding, a modulation, a resounding. A surf, a sea underneath another order. Simultaneously, many narratives moving along; those similar sounds, the year's narrative, one's own..

Poetry, in its finitude, both asks us to make a new realism, somewhat adequate to current complexities, to *be of this time*, and, of necessity, to make choices (and thus to leave some things out). **Scrape up art from surfaces unbidden.** Poetry as an instance of miraculous noticings. In all attention, **I walk away.**

Reading slowly educates us into the text's and reading's own evolving modes of perception. **Apt secrets revealed by looking, instead of looking at, fill my silhouette.**

What would be the record—the form, the words—of **looking, instead of looking at**? And what might we write about such a reading experience? Would it be reading as we have (historically) known (and described) it? **Control's conceit, out of each substance's specificity gobbled, flickers at the idea.** How, in reading, in writing, in publishing, in editing, *not* to control but to engage in a manner that still is of value to others….

Poverty, from my wife and family

separated

for batting, forgiving the very thorns that
wreck my sleep. Longer surviving

figuring it out, troubling the wound to out-
last me. Spar for it. Can codify uncertainty
here in the nearer acreage, albeit inaccurately,
these deities.

To relinquish control, or, to acknowledge the importance of absences which both wound and educate us; in the proximate, in looking, to find those moments of noteworthy uncertainty that we can transmit.

And then the word **condensery**—a Niedecker word (as in the title of her complete writing: *From This Condensery*)? Perhaps also a Zukofsky word? A trace of Pound and *condensare*—

and lyricized sentences. One, the beauty of sound: **Your little peals part, whole scrabble to douser under scrubby sage.** And a compelling and unexpected romanticism: **Until you light, investing the common, redeemable dream.**

This difficulty multiplies a pinpoint phrases, care taken in song's resolve. What is it that song resolves? As the sentence begins recognizably to sing, as the poem begins to sound so, are we marking a particular interval of consciousness, *its* song? As poets, to make a poetry that participates in the beauties of song but not in a manner that merely displays *my* craft nor in a way that succumbs to a merely ornamental or diverting attractiveness.

Cry for a stiff throat, glide to another branch.

To proceed in such a way that does not falsify, does not falsely conclude. The going here measured in sentences: **Try my arms, the height of my hips' measure to sap sentences lacking subject, predicate, equilibrium, a pace implies home, identity, mine determined to undermine a diagram.** The wandering, the sentenced attentiveness, becomes a hunting too: **Sharpen my plan, an image of hunting.**

First to write them, then get to know the less

and less form assuming. Poem to another

auditor: prayer, chant, lecture lovingly as-

sembled. When will you tell me

the time it took to find that skull, to carry it

home. Altar became dumb need for a fly

whisk. More private, all you've written

founded on

volume than blood. Pine needle aloft, a few

yards away, liveforever

my last sight. Scratchings became my left

foot scared awake. Hopping in panic a physi-

cal rag dripping rum

paper to air ignite, abrade my body. Shadow

passing sun passing shadow. I'm here some-

where you're talking to

pace in a circle, scheme, while there is still

light.

In the writing having to risk a breakdown of our modes of knowing *so as not to trivialize writing's relationship to being.* And the poem's act of address too gets risked as the petition becomes less directly manipulative, less and less a recognizable rhetoric. This text is the place I find a Gil Ott I am talking to…. And it is a place where he has incarnated an I that may be that sought place of looking. Momentarily.

2 / 4

Yes, indeed: **What profit from a poem** [.] Certainly not a monetary profit. No one knows *that* better than a small press publisher. As a place, a poem **is many sensate at play, fools surviving in a column of words.** To allow that many to make a site of sensate play, playing at the edge of the sensible, site for foolishness…. Or, that great tranquillity, an emptying out, it is *not* I's story, **and be a part of nothing.**

That sudden beauty, apprised (and prized) in the bulky oddity of almost sensible saying: **Danged friable paths and utter fixed attends a slight sway, a quick glance left and staple on.** Why do we, as readers, as critics, as writers about poetry cling to certain sentences, gathering and making our own anthology from the poet's finite gathered text? News that stays news. In the morning, a day of leisure, reading aloud in amazement to one's beloved a choice morsel of news, the words served up with the coffee and bagels…. The pleasure of judging the sentence pleasurable. The confirmation of that pleasure discerned. Any reading, each reading: a reading of reading. As the writing.

The bobcat had been seen, and verified. And then back into hiding…**a tense identity violating mere whereabouts.** How, then, in such a text, to be here. **The text is nothing, not even writing.** Looking for it, and writing/reading with you.

Not that it can't be, but I can't tell you. In and out of camouflage, momentarily known, then hidden under brush. **Length a day out under camouflage, attributed odors daily twists out of reach.**

I to those I associate adventure and routine, uncertain in memory.

The pace in part kept by heart, beat, by steps taken, pacing. **Walking in silence, at ability joyous, a muscled speech.** Gil's stay in Sausalito, and the text on the page, an attunement. To what? To a specific place and an extended interval of composing consciousness? To read it now, a similar attuning. In sound, as words' music, **the crevice, creek and marsh coincide.** This place of these words. So, **walking still.**

To stay on the track of: **Reading feces artifact customs are traded to dominate, again, to suggest a safe distance.** Waste: a specific clue, idiosyncratic to that textuality. In my reading resounding your tracking, along the tracks of droppings or gatherings of your written trail. Not so much to find you out, Gil, nor to find out about you, but to share in the communal expressing of our many trackings: **I take time writer to sit, remove you to whom magnified parcelling you out teases alterity.** Each of us *is* a **time writer**. Parcelling, and parcelling *out*, fading into that alterity….

3 / 4

An odd track. Written in Sausalito. Gil from Philadelphia. The small book came to me, in Tuscaloosa, from Tenerife. Now, airborne, LA to Dallas, then Dallas to Birmingham, reading, writing…. Resuming, as my time allows, a week later…. **Of use to dead souls**…What is of use to *dead* souls? Among the living? …**resistance turns a minor note**…Which are the minor notes, and where might we find a whole note (major or minor key)? Gil's text has implicitly been a quest and a ritual, though scrupulously *not* formulaic. More in the manner of a phrase I have just received from Kathleen Fraser: *the innovative necessity.*

Gradually, the deed of Gil's text, its/his manner of operation, becomes a little clearer. My recent readings in Maya Deren's *The Divine Horsemen: The Living Gods of Haiti* (which enters into my friend Jake Berry's *Brambu Drezi*) help. **Habiting the stall, inkling who, to whom I'll receive my utilization. Will to erase will be damaged by orthodoxy. Sitting still and complicated beginning, out of us shocked a full life.** Summoning. Writing, attentively, in decomposition. To be ridden. **Always here and now, the inventing looking for itself, and back again fearing and drawn.** (Gil's note at the bottom of the page—the only such note for *The Whole Note*—**W/ thanks to Dr. Louis Mars, *The Crisis of Possession in Voodoo*, Reed, Cannon and Johnson Publishing, 1977.**)

To be written, to be ridden. Not merely as passive medium, not Eliot's filament of platinum, not that catalyst exactly, but an informed, particular, historically and culturally cognizant rite/ person/horse/medium. Through which the *loas* flow and act. One way of thinking about intensive instances of reading and writing. **Half a day spun fenced to burn individual meat, acting out me, the author, the pleasure of every company.** The I become the other; the text-site I make made in fact by a community writing through me. **Cede nothing, I'm separate from penetrate my limbs, cross against my will.** Cross-roads. Writing as the reconciling (and embodying) of polyphony: **Pry with a twig the mass a ready man dances to reconcile sounds from a rural grave with vacant unison.** Not to write some simple unison which would falsify this complex consciousness, but to write the crossings and re-crossings, accurate markings of such noteworthy intervals.

Entry into that site may only be re-told partially: **Noticed but did not record futility in describing the mount, some particle of dirt talking in tongues.** That site both one of fusion and dissolution. **Explaining cartilaginous fuses adequacy, the sitter, thin milled timber smashed contending.** Or, **Fabric rip by singing a dare to the accuser....**

And then the text turns back to discern what has happened, in time to summarize: **Remote home coaxed out of the dark, glossolale to fix it.** Laurie Anderson speaks of a Nerve Bible. Gil's experience: **Residence bone and nerve scuff on purer air.** My own reading becomes a passing over, and a periodic erratic dwelling with. At times, in that movement through and with, I come upon a sentence/site that is remarkable and mystifying, that feels like it has clarity and force, but one to which I have no response: **So it is amnesia// sentences out of youth.** I could hear Dylan sing that in the era of *Highway 61* or *Blonde on Blonde*, and I would nod a similar assent.

The poem then as *passage made*:

                           The hole this morn-

ing fills with trembling made the passage,

marked by all but absent son. Call the scar

your son.

And then left us reading the traces. At this point, the text attends to the inevitable disappearance of that presence:

                       The last hour, caught not

looking for an answer's a kestrel, nesting in

the cornice. Aren't they beautiful answers

which flee their trace. How faster

from which a poem, out of identical anguish.

Lightweight, out of control, moved

to panic, waking late. A convincing wisdom,

walk into the fire. What other choice peeled

off behind me, me again.

What does it mean for an avant garde writing practice to turn toward the realm of the spiritual? If a dominant strand of American innovative poetry has been based (in part) on a critique of prevailing (rather mindless, habitual) rhetorics—for example, rhetorics of personal lyrical epiphany by means of a plainspoken univocal narration with a garnish of tactile imagery—what do we make of *many* fairly recent important writings that decisively *do* enter the realm of the mythic and the spiritual, but that do so with a sustained sense of *innovative necessity*? A few examples (in addition to *The Whole Note*) that come to mind: John Taggart's *Loop* and the forthcoming *Crosses*; Jack Foley's *Exile* and *Adrift*; Jake Berry's *Brambu Drezi* (Books 1 & 2) and his CD *Shadow Resolve*; all of Nathaniel Mackey's work but especially *School of Udhra* and his ongoing *Song of the Andoumboulou*; Tom Mandel's *Prospect of Release*; all of Jerome Rothenberg's work including recent publications such as *Seedings & Other Poems* and *The Book, Spiritual Instrument*; and the compelling writing of zen abbot Norman Fischer, particularly *Jerusalem Midnight* and *Precisely the Point Being Made*. There is also the way that such writings encourage us to re-read (more fully, less through a lens of an implicit set of Do's and Don't's of experimentalism) the work of Paul Celan and Robert Duncan and Hannah Weiner and Emily Dickinson and Larry Eigner and Jack Spicer and many others.

I feel a particular kinship with Gil's *The Whole Note* and the writings of other peers as we exit, in a phrase I e-mailed to Norman Fischer, an avant-garder-than-thou phase. Perhaps as younger writers as we moved decisively away from habitual mainstream practices that we perceived as patently inadequate to what we would do and be and risk in writing, as we adhered to that *innovative necessity*, we may have internalized too rigidly a set of experimental Do's and Don't's that must eventually be themselves supplanted if our writing is ever to enter into its necessary fullness, its full relationship to being. Or, as Norman Fischer e-mailed me in response (October 15, 1998): "yes i think i am in the same place you are—not needing to be so pure in the poetry, but now, after all that, just seeing how to say what is true, with all that behind us—with us and in us." I hear *The Whole Note* in that melodic context.

Each of Gil's four sections consists of eight pages—an eight-page or eight-bar blues? The poem is a touching down, and a flight given temporary incarnation: **Moving, variant ornithography of those uninitiated made into memory by the me briefly incarnate.** An ornithology turned to **variant ornithography**, at the cross-roads of that brief incarnation that I, as a writing self, make and participate in. The writing of Bird. A flight, and a reining in: **Full of myself on successive nights dense and alone sings you back. Need keeps the book of dying open, the language common after all.** I have heard stories about Gil's kidney condition, and find here a broader metaphoric resonance: **adopted to debility**—which I also hear as cousin to *adapted to debility*—as we each do adapt to and are adopted by our abilities and debilities. And, oh, I would love to hear what my friend John Taggart might say about **Christian to these passions without time this time the visitor will burn along forced choice of hosts.**

Thus we each live and write: **Minded the story of a life he'd got foot on, so careful.**

In this particular writing, in *The Whole Note*, Gil writes toward a greater clarity or immediacy of expression of a personal and particular path of activity, all the while making sure that the I of this writing is appropriately displaced, appropriately a medium rather than a heroic individual. If a will is exercised, it is of a more communal nature—writing as the imagining of a collective endeavor for which one is incarnate (somewhat momentarily) as the instance's scribe: **in the round of abnegate scoring among locking peer workers [.]… Wake to me aisle between waking us simultaneously.** To write again, perhaps, of that movement toward waking, as part of many others' writing a kindred chronicle, a writing given over to that innovative necessity **and chance cohesion of mind.**

When we write about the marginalization of poetry, and of the innovative poet's further marginalization, such descriptions implicitly pretend to some dramatic institutional and historical struggle. In fact, the daily writing experience of one committed to the innovative necessity is far less dramatic. **Foretold the under this chair I sit on, humbled and green, and gray…. Scrabble in any direction glory little, like a squirrel.** Theorized tales of marginalization are often full of a compensatory adolescent heroizing of the outlaw and the rebel. As one writes and writes, even one's self presence becomes a rather muted thing: **Piled on every bone felt, and beside me, unexpected, me.** So that, as in the etymology of the word ecstasy, one could be beside oneself. Quite quietly. **What protected artery this weak, human circumstance advances the distance resonance marks.**

We live and write and think among a set of seepages, of forces and memories and writings that move through us: **Fear, but fear's subject unremembered, everywhere present.** I begin to think more and more insistently that poetry provides us with a phenomenology of temporality. In Gil's *The Whole Note*, I locate a grateful writing of that experience (and one which has shed the customary pomposity and self-centeredness of the habitual quest-tale), of poetry as a site for serious uncertainty, for an intensification of being by means of such a testing out:

> Dispassionate grace the water's
>
> edge
>
>
> reach to what hypothesis uncertainty led the
>
> spirit. Still, moving, speaking, incomprehen-
>
> sible. Feet set in mud, decayed, and other
>
> feet
>
>
> tirelessly composed. From lap and slaver
>
> crusts tenuously amid succeeding motilities
>
> endure, some history, any.

Gil's particular tale (this time) is one of renewal—of error, and (quietly) redemption: **I have made a mistake, a meandering stasis, down a notch and starting over.** This four-part story, for which the fourth does contain considerable summary, becomes a reeling from and a reeling in, an assaying: **Fed on seed here, a small black bird far and still admissible.** Crucial to the humbling nature of that experience is a rewriting of writing, a re-initiation into what we write for: **I will build a body of utterance, that fooled me.** One false initiation is into that heroic expectation of building a body of utterance, of, heroically, being a writer of consequence and importance. Gil's new work ends with a self-effaced Whitmanian perspective:

> The odor will stay,
>
> and I
>
>
> will walk away.

Whitman's over-amped posturing, his American egotistical triumphant dissolution becomes, in Gil's writing, a much more muted event. Perhaps a personally distinctive odor lingers, but, quite decisively, that thing called I walks away.

As I read and wrote with Gil's book, I found myself thinking that the mystical quality of poetry is the timing of its timeliness. As a reader, we can rarely determine in advance what it is that we will find to be timely—which read will be formative, which new (or old) poetry will in this instance of reading prove to be peculiarly pertinent or beneficial (or beneficially irritating, or merely irritating). And so with our writing as well. We enter again and again that charged ethical and spiritual place of writing and reading. In this instance, reading and writing in the place of Gil's *The Whole Note*, I have been pleasantly surprised at the particular timing of that timeliness and am grateful for the unexpected clarifications and confusions that have ensued.

Andrew Levy

Paper Blind Blanket

to Gil Ott

dear trouble maker, ideation stays a problem
"& our government" lather (& father) theirs
a rice field, maw, no hands . . . if I am the annointed
one, fuck sublimation. Trampled filter burn through
your buckle hog fresco spectacle matrix husk rub
numerological gist dissatisfaction — take the language
the fourth dimension is in my ass, still lingers
as the haze that represents spring decipher bean
autonomous procedures show us some respect
bridal paths nursed on science fiction what could
have made me think the typical version of love
I've been bathing in the poem, is either impossible
led by a bridle toward the jungle of various
go to saleable slaughter of docility, or conditioning
a lover of beauty who love by debt uncancelled
had sense at meal time to beat up a giraffe's eye
in indestructible ignorance suspected, a glow worm
through the impenetrable stagger to equity
ensheaved and barley corn against sunrise sincere
numerical constitution of each day — nostril
lose against slabs. I have announced my hermitage
the moon will rise in that vicinity, the neglected hoe
fills my top in such loveliness infants become
too troublesome after sex, mealed movements
swell with memories that prevented their being
tracked away from home — yet it seems readied
that those heavenly music or demi-gods in

recognition a mere hog eating one another

comes in their cruelty, plummet every sound

the size of a pin the folds of master and monkey

radiating all perpetual dullness with fullness

But you like none, none you, no fish will swim

and play wantonly dressing old words new

form & bend the style the young man's courting,

no stone cut smooth unknown in its end

and place someone you do not know

necessity only thin ice in thaw desperate physic

dark as night and brought back objective

glimmering with light a world of certainty

the facts merge in the poetry; whom can I unburden

that the drama can lend burn and freeze

beauty if doubt is god's mouth, the autumn sleeve

comes on distinctly, it made you that table

all that it retains — miscellaneous residencies

distantly connected, respect to despise defect

the insects named kept in a tub

goes on writing poems (the water ceasing to drip)

yields to stillness every good think is called

that covers all, that covers all, but the language

and imagery stretch the deserted not to be

concert hall or small butt, the prolongation

in the quality of friends is not especially elevated

the person loving reveals the fact in the face

suffers cruel restraint, "how I hide my love"

those who cross mountains or hills

a word association with "sane," would disjoint

"do I not spend my self respect?" warrant

the trojan hours, the quick experiment gone awry?

He would rid himself of life, his desires

take over the world for a select few

frankensteins do not brush away, do not delay

are distinctions to aggravate "my world"

but "ours" includes that, so does this world

all dates approximate, real and non-existent

ruining the grain, beating the clothes, the big

monster's errors implants in our brains

or that one might lose one's entire life

have it retreat twenty years into the past

an experiment gone awry unbuttoning

its hands disperse the necessities, recline

where it should, "all echoes link as air"

— an envelopment, 3/2/98, 10:15-11:51 p.m.

Chris McCreary

Review of *Drunkard Boxing*,
the first product of Gil Ott's Philadelphia Publishing Project

Linh Dinh's chapbook, *Drunkard Boxing*, marks the beginning of a new era for Gil Ott's Singing Horse Press. *Drunkard Boxing* is the first publication of the Philadelphia Publishing Project; each year, the Project will publish the work of a Philadelphia poet with, in Ott's words, "little or no print exposure, yet deserving of a national audience." It is fitting that, in the midst of such a proliferation of new publishing projects taking place in and around Philadelphia (BeautifulSwimmer Press, *COMBO*, handwritten records & books, *ixnay/ixnay press*, *pH*, the *Philly Talks* newsletter) that it is Ott's Singing Horse Press that initiates such a worthwhile project capable of reaching such a large and diverse audience.

Drunkard Boxing is an often jarring read that melds moments of extreme violence with a language of detached description and staccato commands. The opening poem, "Laced Farina," reads like an off-kilter catechism, with the litany of romantic or sexual questions, "Who touched your hair?" only half answered by replies steeped in the language of war, "A rifle butt to the side of the head." As the poem progresses, the division between sex and violence is erased, and the action is "like fireworks. One is thrown in the air... One is undressed by the whizzing bullets." Brutality is eroticized and sex is cast as a harsh, hollow act, leaving the reader on an uneven, uneasy ground.

Violence, or, more specifically, violation, occurs in different forms throughout the poems. It seems that women especially must constantly be on their guard. The nature of the exact threat is not always made clear, and it is more frightening and sinister because of that ambiguity: a woman seeking shelter in a foxhole, for example, feels something touching her from behind and cannot be sure if it is a hand or a hand grenade. In the context of these poems, it is irrelevant, as both are only mechanisms of destruction. In these poems, men "chok(e) intentions in a flourish of tenderness."

While the first poems in the collection deal more specifically with a land that is literally under siege, later poems shift their focus geographically to a different landscape that is, in many ways, just as bleak. "The Dead" points to the immigrants who are the urban outcasts of the western world, those who "sit at formica tables smoking discount cigarettes. / Some have dyed their hair, some have changed their name to Bill."

> The old lady who scrounged potted meat
>
> From foreign men lying in a mortar pit

Now sells gold jewelry in Santa Barbara.

The dead are not dead but wave at pretty strangers

From their pick-up trucks on Bolsa Avenue.

The "dead," then, have fled one war zone and have shed their old identities only to find themselves in the midst of another, less clearly defined battle.

At the center of many of these poems are the labored, claustrophobic gestures of the human body. Sexual couplings not charged with the language of war progress with a stilted, futile air reminiscent of the incremental movements of Beckett's later prose. The terse, tough language of these poems, though, moves with an understated grace in the midst of lands and bodies laid waste. The narrative voice is constantly searching for a way to coax beauty from this oblivion: "Don't say, 'The bullet yawed / inside the body.' Say, "The bullet danced inside the body.""

The carnage should not be ignored or turned away from in disgust, then. Perhaps the only answers to be found here are those that can be arrived at after passing through the minefield of the poems. As stated in the poem "Traditional Vietnamese Architecture," "An entry should always be / illicit. Unobstructed entrances are not worth passing through."

Linh Dinh, *Drunkard Boxing*. (Singing Horse Press, 1998, 36 pp., $8.00, ISBN 0-9350162-18-6. For more information on the Philadelphia Publishing Project, or to order *Drunkard Boxing*, write to: Singing Horse Press, P.O. Box 40034, Philadelphia PA 19106.)

Toby Olson

Calling Forth The Poem

> I am calling forth a poem.
> I am calling forth a poem.

> Come help me sing the song.
> Come be with me the poem.

The Public Domain is Philadelphia, and I remember our first meeting shortly after I arrived here in 1975. I'd been looking for connection in this new city. Connection to poetry, not the politics of it, with no luck.

The room was like a solarium. Was it a hospital? The University of Pennsylvania? We talked about poetry then, intensely, various positionings and searches, those whose work we'd loved. It was something I'd been missing; maybe he had too. I was on the brink of fiction then, and Gil I think was getting ready to get ready for his own journey, at least it seems that way in memory. Nathaniel Tarn had mentioned that we should get together. Or Eli Goldblatt had. Or maybe it was John Taggart. Or Gil had called me on the phone. Or I had called him. Memory fails, but I remember the room and circumstance, talking at the brink of something of unquestioned value.

And in this intimate city there has seemed no need for letters over the years, just word of mouth, like poetry, and yet there's a letter tucked in my copy of *The Whole Note*: "Thanks so much for your considerate... Wanted to send the enclosed, just out and rare."

> from which a poem, out of identical anguish.
> *Lightweight, out of control, moved*

Nor many phone calls either over the years, and yet Gil's presence in my mind and in the life of poetry in this city remains constant. Not only poems, but always of the spirit that produces his: community arts work at the Painted Bride, his helping me with a planned world-music concert, one that never materialized but his spirit in it all the way. There were and are the Robin's celebratory readings, those earlier on at McGlinchey's Bar, Gil popping in and out, a few moments of intensity, laughter and knowingness. And there are always his publications too, his poetry and his service to poetry with Singing Horse Press, *Paper Air*. I think it's fair to say that life in the delicate muscularity of poetry, beneath the politics of poetry, in this city, owes much of its vitality to Gil. Beyond this city too of course, but I'm not speaking of that. Perhaps no other poetry I can read here answers better to Creeley's stern injuction: "The poem supreme, addressed to / emptiness—..."

> Two men's faces
> in the night

in the doorway

red.

But we were in a car and heading west in little traffic. It was 1978, I think it was his car, but I remember driving, so perhaps it was mine. Headed to Shippensburg and John Taggart, reading another's poetry. Something about that, even a better sharing than reading one's own. The poem was Taggart's "Peace on Earth," a long monstrosity of a poem, a prayer even. We'd be interviewing him, Gil would, and I'd be taking some photographs. In Taggart's house it was another thing, but in the car, reading those stanzas aloud — *I am calling forth a poem....Come help me sing the song.* — some communal offering, being together there as poets, speaking from paper into air. This, I remember vividly. Perhaps

brief dust accumulated a test of senses only,

were failed. Noticed but did not record

recorded here.

How have the years gone by? We see each other occasionally. I saw Gil in the hospital recently. Gil's poetry and his presence have helped to make this city as much of a human place as it might be, tangibly. I went into fiction thoroughly shortly after that trip to Taggart's. I didn't see Gil for quite a while then. He was finding his own, and his various publications came to me, their beauty of a different kind. My vector was another. Still, talking, we could always talk, richer, more human than politics or aesthetics.

This last summer, playing golf on the Cape, I'd hit a perfect draw, bringing the ball in from the right; my partner's was a cut shot, a fade. Different travels from a common source, but the balls landed very close together two hundred yards out. They rested there, in advance of our arrival, like poetry as yet unwritten. They were white, in the grass and clear air, only later to be taken into memory,

opaque. Without me, you..

Gil, we could have dropped a hat over them.

Bob Perelman

Letter to Gil

D
ear Gil, I w

onder where
the dail

y
noises st
art making

poetry hap
pen hap
py
or not read

y to c
ontinue being what they on
ce sounded like the
y
were starting out to say being one thing being another sound in min

d if you believe t
hat then here's *T*
he Brid
ge
I want you to put
a down payment on

just a wor
d or t
wo and the span wil
l stand i
n space
for as long

as you continue to a

id its long le

ngth or was that

its st

rong st

rength in upl

ifting our ne

ural pathways if you

know what's go

od for you th

en you kn

ow wh

at you kn

ow and

if you do

n't then wha

t you kn

ow is so

mething else

on a distan

t altitude relea

sing

lines

from the ch

armed st

age of

melod

ious incipience

we wa

n

t to h

ear

the pie

ce am

id

the war

of no
is
es.

Y
ours,

Bob

Leslie Scalapino

For Gil Ott

A while ago Gil proposed a collaboration between Norman Fischer, Alan Davies, and myself on the subject of, or responding to, *Influence of Eastern Thought*. Although I began the collaboration, so far I haven't been able to continue. It seemed hard to write it, though I think his conception of it (subject and collaboration) was very interesting. The influence is event. I would like to give this poem in response to Gil's sense of what that exchange could be about. This was written prior to the collaboration, in a work called *New Time*. For Gil:

      we can not speak as to concentrate on the constructed unit — nor sleep much and that 'causes' (?) an actual harmony, serial or it's there after a while, not based on the similarities of the people

    the night is exhaustion rains

    luminous night while running to the rise

    that's dawn is when running to the rise, later

    the rise is the floating people

Kerry Sherrin

Intersections

for Gil Ott
I will build a body of utterance, that
fooled me.

from *The Whole Note*

Every day a new system seemed possible.

money

I was twenty and wanted to be a poet.

certainly

With another woman, who was older and knew more about contemporary poetry, I ran a
reading series called Fresh Fish at the University of Pennsylvania.

love

Penn was dominated by the Reaganites in those years.

maybe

The future bankers disdained the poets yet secretly yearned to be so artsy and irresponsible
and free of the compulsion to go to law school.

blood

The poets disdained the future financiers while secretly banking on their own apparent
iconoclasm as though it might be a guarantee.

words

I went to fraternity parties and compared SAT scores with guys I sometimes slept with later.

bent

If they were cute, I wanted to. If they weren't, I usually didn't.

him

I'm on my way to work at Penn.

As part of our series we published a monthly calendar of readings, and we brought feminist and formally experimental poets to Penn.

    back.

      I'm late — speeding as usual.

Secretly I wondered if any of these living poets would be, could be great.

    two   lines

        It's the winding part of the drive through a neighborhood of stone mansions and wide driveways.

I knew it was about greatness even though I couldn't say what it was to be great, exactly.

    crooked

      He's walking along — is it him — it is — along the edge of the road.

Something to do with books—with the thickness of them, even.

    even

      I pull off onto a side street and wait for him to reach the corner, then open my window.

I thought I knew everything I'd need to know to discern things from each other, eventually.

    Straight

      "I couldn't tell if you were you."

He worked at the Painted Bride.

    as a story

      "I was thinking, who is this beautiful woman."

I'd heard his name from my friend.

    about

His wrists are frail, his body slightly bent.

He gave me copies of *Paper Air*.

     him

        He's wearing green pants, a beige shirt.

I took a course in arts management and interviewed him for my final project.

     and me.

        He's carrying a tote bag.

He explained that he'd been very ill and had needed the most urgent sort of help from his family.

     luuuuuv

        It looks heavy, bulges at the bottom.

He was neither brash nor neurasthenic, unlike the other male writers whom I'd met or about whom I'd read.

     may   be

        Books, it turns out, new books.

I was surprised he had no wife.

     money

        He hands me a copy of this latest book, of poems by a writer who lives here in Philadelphia.

He didn't have a lot of money, I didn't think.

     whirrrds

        He says he lives up the hill.

I spent a month on the report.

     bent

        There isn't anyone, there isn't.

I didn't know anyone else like him.

      forward.

            No one.

He might have liked me.

      Two lines

            Like him.

Liked me, that's how we all said it.

      back.

            The light changes to green.

I hardly noticed.

      Or an even

            He hoists his bag.

The report was graded at the end of the semester.

      three.

            "In my head as I drove away."

Can't find the transcript.

      who was   who

            Hey. Hey!

It never occurred to me I'd be in his book.

      were   they

            Glad to. Glad to see your face.

Ron Silliman

Blue

For Gil Ott

The Marchioness went out at five o'clock. The sky was blue yet tinged with pink over the white spires which broke up the east horizon. The smell of the afternoon's brief shower was still evident and small pools of clear water collected in the tilt of the gutters, leaves and tiny curling scraps of paper drifting in the miniature tides which nonetheless caught and reflected the swollen sun, giving the boulevard its jeweled expression.

Government was therefore an attitude. Dour, the camel pushed with his nose against the cyclone fence. The smell of damp eucalyptus is everything! You stare at your car before you get in.

From here we can see the sex. They are folding the flyers before stuffing them into envelopes. Badminton is nothing to be ashamed of. Grease and old tire marks streak the road. From here we can tell the sex.

Rust designs that old truck door. The number of objects is limited. Some leaves on the fern are more yellow. Sooner or later you will have to get up to change the record. That buzz is the dryer.

Longer ones demand a new approach: there's not enough water for a second cup. These crystals are useless on a sunless day. More than that, the fence is apt to give, pulling free of its posts. Tell me the one about the fellaheen again.

It's a trap: they want you to think that light is Venus. Under a microscope we see them absorb their elders. A spider plant is only one design. I took the message.

At dusk, very little is neutral. The corner merchant, a quiet Persian, nods to her as she waits for a break in the traffic. Those who are not consigned to the prolonged concentration of driving have already fallen asleep. At the intersection the sidewalks are rounded.

The flower closes slowly about the unsuspecting fly. The thickness of the gum limits the rhythm of his chewing. Wasn't he happy here, viewing clip after clip of that old successful launch? The glove compartment never held a glove, nor I.

So you go faster, hunched over, avoiding the headlines in the boxes. The taller buildings suck the wind. That butter only appears to be firm, the hood never will quite shut. Between what were once squares of concrete, anonymous weeds bunch & spread.

If challenged, its first response is to spit. This took place at the museum. Wires slope from the pole to the house, where they gather, entering a narrow pipe along its side. This conveys motion. I am writing in shadows. Don't you worry about accessibility too?

Mother simply likes to have the books. Like a serenade, only earlier. He lets the clay on his hands begin to dry. Fuchsia blossoms stain the walk, the doorknob strangled by rubber bands. Another thing, pepper is not a corn.

So what is despair? The cyclist trapped inside her helmet? The girl sent to the grocer for milk? The moment before? The mops on the old porch have begun to dissolve. Don't turn the light on till you get the shade. Atop a small house, the cartoon dog types away. Turn the page.

Shorter is. The fern sits, its clay pot in a pool of water. In doubles, that's called poaching. The back of the television faces the window. From here you can smell the sex. Give those socks a little more time. More narrow.

At the arched door of the restaurant she checks her watch, a delicate gold bracelet dangling from her wrist. Bands of a deep orange streak a near purple sky, the brisk air shuddering in the small trees, slender branches bending back. Children begin to gather up their toys; lights on, their homes begin to glow. The host, recognizing the Marchioness, invites her in.

Chris Stroffolino

The Politics of Poetic Form and its (Dis)contents: Some Thoughts on Gil Ott

The final issue of *Paper Air* (Volume 4, Number 3), the journal Gil Ott edited from 1976 to 1990, includes a prefatory statement by Gil that serves as both a self-critical "assessment of [his] own energies" as an editor, writer, and community activist, as well as a proactive manifesto of sorts that challenges some of the guiding assumptions of the political and social efficacy of contemporary avant-garde poetry — particularly the *L=A=N=G=U=A=G=E* group, with whom Ott had been affiliated in an often uneasy alliance. This statement, appearing years before the controversial *Apex of the M* editorials, before Bob Perelman's and Barrett Watten's similar challenges to the social efficacy of radical disjunction and its emphasis on "the material text," may be seen in retrospect as a courageous wake-up call to writers who — however earnestly — have been duped into believing that "the most radical writing and reading strategies are ... sufficient, by themselves, to effect cultural transformation." (Ott, 5)

In this essay, we see Ott going beyond such positions expressed in the very same issue of *Paper Air*. This can be seen most clearly if we contrast the final essay in this issue, Bruce Andrews' "Poetry as Explanation, Poetry as Praxis," with the position to which Ott arrives. According to Andrews:

> Conventionally, radical dissent & "politics" in writing would be
> measured in terms of communication & concrete effects on an
> audience...The usual assumptions about unmediated communication,
> giving "voice" to "individual" "experience," the transparency of
> the medium (language), the instrumentalizing of language,
> pluralism, etc. bedevil this project. But more basically: such
> conventionally progressive literature fails to self-examine
> writing & its medium, language.... [I]t can't really make claims to
> comprehend and/or challenge the nature of the social whole; it
> can't be political in that crucial way. (103)

For Andrews, "the need to see society as a whole" is best served by "a conception of writing *as* politics, not writing *about* politics" (103). While Ott may, to some extent, share Andrews' views (after all, he was the first to publish this piece which has since been republished in *The Politics of Poetic Form* and excerpted in *The Norton Anthology of Postmodern Poetry*), we do Ott an injustice if we fail to emphasize the ways in which his essay challenges Andrews' core assumptions. Ott claims:

> In editing recent issues of *Paper Air*, I have sought what I called
> — awkwardly — evidence of "social engagement", or "the political"
> in contributions. The difficulty of this qualification, when the
> dominating positions in American poetics either reduce the
> possibilities of content to a precious exaltation of individual
> perception and closure (=signature=ownership), or, at an
> "opposite" pole (yet with a similar effect), champion formal
> disruption *as* political strategy, has yielded slow progress. (5)

While Ott shares with Andrews a skepticism towards what Andrews terms "the usual assumptions about unmediated communication, giving 'voice' to 'individual' 'experience'," he reveals his "resistance to dogma" and his heroic "independence from professional or other market-driven affiliation" by coming to the position that his editorial direction must require "*in advance of* aesthetic considerations, ethnic and sexual diversity, insistently attended, to challenge the racism and sexual paranoia rampant with the mix." For an editor who increasingly came to publish non-white, non-male, even non-"avant-garde" poets, writers, and photographers, this is no idle statement (and where else in the late 80s and early 90s, do we find a journal with "avant-garde" "credentials" that also publishes Ahmad Dahbour, Lamont Steptoe, Ammiel Alcalay, Harryette Mullen, Kofi Natambu, Edgar Heap of Birds, Israel Torres Penchi, and others?) There is the implication — in Ott's essay — that even Andrews has hocked "the art's best argument against charges of elitism or solipsism, for the flaccid xenophobia and machismo which characterize American society and language." (5)

Furthermore, it is important to recognize that Ott, after ceasing publication of *Paper Air* in 1990 (though he continued to write his own poetry and publish Singing Horse Press) actively stepped-up his social activism in a broader social arena. In addition to his activities at the Painted Bride Arts Center (which often went beyond the call of professional duty), he worked closely with artists and activists involved with The Taller Puertorriqueño and the Ife Ife Center in North Philadelphia. The closest precedents and analogies I find for Ott's activity here are with Amiri Baraka and Frantz Fanon. Baraka, for instance, after operating largely in (and attempting to share the aesthetic assumptions of) the sophisticated white "middle-class" avant-garde bohemian milieu of the late 1950s and early 1960s (such as Charles Olson and Frank O'Hara), came up against the limits of his participation in such a world. Although his involvement in the avant-garde sophisticated literary scene of his day may have conferred on him a "fame" and a cultural "authority" Ott has not as of yet achieved, Baraka heroically risked ostracism from this elite to "cash in" on his notoriety to become a populist performer, poet, and cultural critic (and one actively involved in Newark politics for over 30 years). Likewise, Fanon, after achieving success among European intellectual elites for his early Lacan-inflected *Black Skin, White Masks*, came — in his later writing and social activities — to turn his back on the sophisticated complications of social binaries (such as race and class) that characterized this book.

The examples Baraka, Fanon, Cesaire, and Ott have set help dramatize the ways in which an intellectual and activist can "grow up in public" and come to a realization that the sophisticated "alternative" to "mainstream" or "common-sense" thinking may, if viewed ethically rather than aesthetically, work within the same bourgeois assumptions it claims (whether through ignorance or willful obfuscation) to oppose. I have no doubt that Ott himself — as an early and consistent proponent and practitioner of "language writing" in the 1980s (though one who nevertheless maintained an interest in raw orality, and who often sang poems by the Bay Area poet "Kush" at his readings) — genuinely believed for a time in the liberating potentials of such methods. Yet, it is significant that he would come to a point where he could no longer agree with Andrews that it is a "convention" in American Poetry that writing be used to "communicate" and achieve "a concrete effect" on its readers. There is a rigorous self-questioning as well as a proletarian didacticism in Ott's best public work (see, for instance, his poem "Status") that, unfortunately, is as out of place in Andrews' recipe for the properly political poem as it is in the "show don't tell" aesthetics of "mainstream" American poetry. It is high time that Gil Ott receives his due as a heroic harbinger who's shown how one need not reject writing *about* politics (in a way that may be derided as "vulgar" by certain avant-gardistes) in order to reject the bourgeois dogma of the depoliticized experience-oriented American "workshop" lyric.

Mark Wallace

Magic Words: Gil Ott's *The Whole Note*

I had seen over several years many fine pieces of poetry and fiction by Gil Ott — especially the oblique, disjointed, but hauntingly exact work in *The Yellow Floor*, and some outright terrifying (if quietly so, and all the more terrifying for that) short stories in an issue of the journal *To*. Gil's talent was an open secret among my D.C. Area poetry friends; Joe Ross in particular had since my arrival in D.C. in 1994 talked frequently of Gil and the influence he had on Joe and others. But it wasn't until the publisher of Zasterle Press, Mañuel Brito, sent me Gil's Zasterle Book *The Whole Note* that I discovered the amazing subtlety that Gil could create in a long poem.

Like pretty much all of Gil's work, *The Whole Note* seems almost to stagger under the burden of past disasters, both self-created and culturally imposed. A great deal of power and danger lurks in the book's taut silences, careful shifts, and elliptical leaps. The tension between language and silence creates what I might call a "landscape of experience"— neither pastoral or conventionally autobiographical, the book nonetheless traces the twists and turns of particular experiences in particular environments. In a note that Gil wrote me in February 1998 about my review of *The Whole Note* that had appeared in *The Washington Review*, he let me know many details behind the book's composition:

> It is interesting to me that you struggle with what the book is "about." I've never made any secret of the fact (though very few have ever asked me!) that it came from a period of intense saturation in a natural environment (the Headlands Center on the Marin coast, where I had a three-month residency in 1990), which led to prolonged meditation on the conflict and reconciliation of socialized and natural being. My study at the time was voodoo, santeria and African American mysticism in general, so social being was reflected as ritual and grotesque symbology, while the "natural"— always a projection — was observed.

In *The Whole Note*, the ritual and grotesque symbology of the social writhes with an unavoidable if often understated horror. And while the specifics of Gil's studies at the time do not show themselves directly in the text, nonetheless the lines foreground a tension that brings language alive as a kind of magic spell designed to uncover the roots of experience.

But experience in *The Whole Note* is not a sequence of events and feelings about them (there's nothing like "when I was a boy, I hated going to school"). Rather, it is a magically charged, material surface of language that reflects, and reflects on, experiences perhaps too elusive to be directly described:

and express my will his habits contemn my

knowledge of his failing

exposed. In his ease those listening as well, a

board stick jammed where bone had been,

the crown of a tooth

spat blood, or rum, collapsing, then standing

again. The steps, once lost, are never ex-

hausted. The youthful look a drug deserts

wants in, that is, out with me, from here.

These lines seem haunted by events they never quite portray, replacing descriptive details with thoughts about experience that are as incomplete as understanding always is. One could attempt to construct personal narrative from such lines, and come to the conclusion that the writer is wrestling with a relation to an alcoholic, perhaps a father, perhaps himself. But the lines don't say that, and can't be made to — experience remains at a remove, except for the experience of language itself. And despite what seems the calm precision of the book's language, these lines and many others are filled with darkness and pain. *The Whole Note* is not the work of a complacent craftsman, but of a powerfully human voice testing the bounds of what language can help him understand, or not understand, as the case may be.

In that same letter to me, Gil spoke of his own sense of the relation between language and experience in the book:

> But I am a poet, so magic plain and simple was my medium. By this I mean chant and the illusion of meaning conjured by the play of the words themselves. My subjects provide sufficient detail; the physical qualities of language grab hold of the attentive reader.

> The magic of a fully embodied language that *is* experience replaces the idea that words describe experiences that exist outside them.

The Whole Note is divided into four sections, titled "1/4," "2/4," "3/4," and "4/4" respectively; obviously, the four sections comprise "the whole note" of Ott's poetic landscape. There is no clear progression or development along the four sections; this is not a book about how to draw conclusions, but rather about responsiveness to the twists and turns of the moment of composition. The book does seem, especially towards the end, often to be a love poem, motivated deeply by loss:

> Full of myself on successive nights
>
> dense and alone sings
>
>
> you back. Need keeps the book of dying
>
> open, the language common after all.

However, while the book's dedication "This book is for Julia" solidifies the impression of love as a central concern, it must be pointed out that nothing in the lines above is certainly directed towards a single person — the "you" in question could equally be a group of others existing in a "language common after all."

The Whole Note presents a poetic voice whose scars are real: "I have made a mistake, a meandering / stasis, down a notch and starting over." But invoking the magic of language does not seem in any simple sense a healing act, at least if one means by healing an attempt to resolve and put behind one the pain that prompted the original invocation. By the end of *The Whole Note*, no containment of self or text is achieved, no resolution offered. The voice remains, as before, jolted by uncertainty:

> I will build a body of
>
> utterance, that fooled me. The odor will stay,
>
> and I
>
>
> will walk away.

Still, a kind of understanding has been found, if only in the recognition that understanding always has limits, but people continue living nevertheless. In walking away from an environment where he never could have stayed, the poet remains open to magic and experience. Fragile, never unified, but determined to live, the voice in *The Whole Note* offers itself to readers as a kind of communion, as evidence of a life that, despite intense pain, has still been realized in writing.

Correspondences

Kristen Gallagher & Gil Ott

Over the course of putting this tribute together, many emails were exchanged. At the end, some of the exchange seemed worth editing to create a piece for the book.

Kristen Gallagher: One thing I want to ask you about is your connection to activism and/or work in what might be called social services. Can you tell me about some of the activism you've been involved in? Why have you chosen the kinds of jobs you have, and for those who don't know — what have some of those jobs been? What relationship has this had with your poetic work?

Gil Ott: The linkage between art and social change is as deeply rooted as it is tenuous. Personally, this contradiction has dogged all my work. Writing, language, the praise terms that predominate are "transparent," "seamless," "unobtrusive," etc. To be an artist who works with language is to have your hands on a great secret, an illusion. It is truly the source of power in our world. And there are no forms of language that have not contributed to some abuse of power. This realization set me out early on, looking for incorruptible forms. The equation was: *disruption of the illusion* = *exposure of the abuse*. Some time ago, however, I realized that this is a mighty big prescription for poetry.

In the 70's and 80's, my poetry 'n' activism took direct forms: street readings, declamations, spray painted protests, etc. There's a role in political activism for poetry, and it can be one that isn't smothered by ideology. You can't have a political movement without art, but the difficulty for the artist, or at least it's been my difficulty, is that art can only be part of the movement. The contradiction is one of vision, the artist's vision ultimately comes into conflict with any political or social program. I can say that in my lifetime I've tried several ways of resolving this crisis, from building alternative publishing and performance venues, to promoting community-based artmaking as an organizing tool.

As for jobs, I have to admit that I haven't chosen them, they've chosen me. The whole notion of being a "professional" is outside my ken. I have two skills. I can write, and I can bring people together around an idea. Beyond that, I've only got limitations, the main one being an abhorrence of any work that I don't entirely believe in. I currently work with people with disabilities. I've surprised myself how well I've made the transition. But these are folks whose goal is to shut down all the nursing homes, to make society good on its promise to accept them as full citizens. They're getting thrown into jail pursuing what is, in a very real sense, a life and death agenda. The disability rights movement is very exciting right now, and makes the artistic avant-garde look downright Republican. I'm learning about this struggle, and I'm proud to be a part of it.

Poetry is one of the oldest and most fundamental forms of expression. It is available to everyone, a way of figuring out the world. As poets, we need to think inclusively, and embrace all sincere effort. I have always believed that poetry, and the arts in general, generate and depend upon community, even when analyzed on the microscopic level of speaker/auditor.

KG: I like this — working with language as working with a great secret, or illusion, a source of power. In your work, and through things you have said, it seems possible that you might believe language-based disruption acts as more of what Leslie Scalapino says is a "self-detonating device" through which one becomes open to approach the social more clearly, with more of an orientation to ethical process, uncertainty. This seems to have the potential outcome that might have very much to do with why you do the work you do (poetic and day-job). I know that the piece Leslie submitted for this book originated from a request made by you that she, Norman Fischer, and Alan Davies collaborate on a work regarding the influence of Eastern thought. Do you feel that Eastern thought, Zen Buddhism in particular, informs your work?

GO: That term — self-detonating device — has great rhetorical appeal. It does not surprise me that it's Leslie's originally. It sounds cathartic, "cleansing the doors of perception," permitting the speaker to embrace the social. Is the poem used up, then, in the detonation? We have to face the fact that the self is as much a fantasy as the social. And if there's a lesson to be learned from the 20th century, it's that anything mass-societal is undesirable. I would be more inclined to agree with Gary Snyder, who speaks of the temporality of communities. They form, around crises, ideas, opportunities, they are small by nature, and they dissolve.

All I could say of the relation of Zen to my writing is that Zen is essentially a practice, sitting, breathing. I have done these things, when I was younger, but now find that discipline only erratically. Writing for me is meditative, both play and struggle. Articulation arrived at is fulfilling, though I don't think that is the point of Zen practice. I am uncomfortable trying to point at something, recognizing "the finger is not the moon."

KG: What I really want to get at is this: how does what you choose to DO for paid employment feed back into your poetic work? I understand what you mean about the artistic avant-garde looking downright Republican. I wonder if you, as activist, being in the neighbor-hood of Kensington, arguably the most troubled area of this city, as opposed to being in an academic/critic atmosphere, keeps your art and the artist yourself more in dialogue with some more troubling aspects of American socio-economics. I just wonder, knowing what I know of the neighborhood you work in, because I have lived there, about what you experi-ence in the line of day-job work you've chosen, and how it might manifest in your poetry? But please tell me if I am pushing too hard on the wrong buttons.

GO: I don't want to make any inflated claims for myself/my "political" involvements, and I don't want to make any for poetry. Nor do I want to come off sounding cynical. To begin, the conflict I described — between the vision of the artist and any social "program" — is not the artist having a conflict with the political, but with the program. One of the most prevalent political applications of poetic language is in the production of rhetoric. This I resist. We poets pay too dearly for our freedom, and I am saddened when I find one of us who accepts the confines of ideology, even when it is an ideology of identity or culture. If there were a politic of poetry, it would be anarchy, or indeterminacy (to borrow from Majorie Perloff). But take that work to, say, Kensington, and you are immediately faced with the grit of community organizing, that people need, say, to learn to read, or write a letter of protest to a bank. You are faced with the question of use, and it is in answering that question — which is first and foremost a personal question — that poetry finds its place in a political movement.

Poetry does have remarkable educational potential, and there is a definite, incremental, empowering element to that. The example of Paolo Frieri is one that all poets should become familiar with, if only to shed the self-revelatory tone that dominates today. Locally, I think of Craig Czury or Homer Jackson, who have gone into prisons and actually changed peoples' lives by helping inmates write their first poems. Or Susan Stewart, who has conducted literacy workshops in Germantown using advanced — but, you'll agree, highly relevant — texts like Harryette Mullen's Muse & Drudge.

As I'm sure I've said, poetry has great community-forming properties, but it's strength is in its admission of multiple views. In this capacity, it can contribute to an organizing program, but it cannot formulate one.

Interestingly, a watershed moment for me as a "political poet" came in 1987, when I visited Nicaragua with a group of writers. The Sandinistas were in power at the time, and they presented themselves as poet/leaders. During the overthrow of Somoza, they had even used the poetry column in the main newspaper in Managua, La Prensa, to encode and communicate military messages! Poetry was being put to a lot of uses: to instill national pride, to promote hard work, even to promote good personal hygiene. The more "artistic" poets, such as Ernesto Cardenal, had to move as far as they could from doctrine, to speak of abstractions like freedom or courage, or to speak in barely-clothed metaphor, and the work suffers for the association. The experience made me realize that the real political work that needs doing is here, in Philadelphia, in the community where I have my own life-or-death stake. And it has less to do with me writing/reading/speaking poetry than it has to do with my finding and encouraging others to do so. Thus the implied bifurcation, and the consequent yearning to patch it up.

I doubt that I'm satifying you with these answers, but they are mine. I have done some work in Kensington, through the Taller Puertorriqueno, the Norris Square Neighborhood Project, and others with which I've had a long association, but I'm sure my stake there is much less than yours.

It seems you need to go back to Kensington to find your answer.

KG: Well, I don't mean to make you out to be some sort of hero. I am interested in discussing what it is like to be a poet and work in this country, at this time, especially when working with groups of people who face more immediate, daily living uncertainties than perhaps you or I do. In addition, being in an atmosphere where vernacular, it's constant shifting of terms, is the respected dialect, while the language of the state is approached with automatic suspicion, and experienced as coercive force.

You were on PBS recently, walking across the Benjamin Franklin Bridge. The poetic monologue, called "Heaven," you say right before you begin, is from a struggling person, a person struggling to voice. The result is not unlike the difficult voicings of many in the homeless population, many of whom, in Philadelphia and all over the US, ended up on the street because of cuts in care for mental health which resulted in the closing of many large institutions. You introduce the piece by saying "a poem is never made by a poet — it is made by the listeners." The movement of the piece and what you say beforehand, makes me think that a listener's attempt to understand the language of the monologue is a way in to get a listener to maybe really listen to someone struggling, that there is a level of understanding possible there, if a listener can relax expectations and just listen. Can you talk about this? I know you don't want to make great claims for poetry's political or social effectiveness — neither do I. However, why do you do this? Why dress up in raggedy clothing and do this kind of monologue on tv? I will say it was quite effective. My mother watched it and said, "you didn't tell me he was homeless."

This seems to me such an important quality that much of your work shares. It is especially up front in *The Whole Note,* where language is a rough terrain where words and sounds come together in a way that foregrounds texture — not unlike walking in the Marin Headlands, as Kevin Killian has pointed out in his piece for this book, where you were when working on *The Whole Note* — one can walk, and it seems pretty and easy from a distance, but once you are negotiating it you realize it is quite treacherous. The walker loses composure, to say the least. This especially resonates when in *The Whole Note* the paragraph/sections just suddenly seem to jut or twist or get lobbed off. And since *The Whole Note* is concerned with the social body meeting the natural body, perhaps poetry's ineffectiveness is somehow the reality of these losses of composure? Perhaps the social body is constantly needing to reorient itself as nature lobs off the possibility of following one thread or path, sending birds to eat breadcrumbs so that we never get "home."

GO: Whew! That's a question full of answers!

The WHYY piece (it was produced by the local PBS affiliate) has been an eye-opener for me. Many, many people have told me they've seen it and liked it. I actually believe that as a piece of performance, it has contributed to peoples' awareness and concern for the homeless.

I cannot, however, divorce that writing from its voicing, nor, much more importantly, from its media presentation. The struggle to articulate, the stuttering, the abrupt breaks, these present the kind of alienation you're talking about, they require the listener to struggle too, to make sense. These effects were amplified by the use of tape recorded voiceovers and ambient sounds. But I think the whole proposal — which is a difficult one — was made palatable by the visuals, the spare beauty of that trip over the bridge. The effect on radio would be entirely different, as would that of live performance. On the page, I'm not sure people have patience for a poem like that.

Your question about the language of the state being experienced as coercive force makes me think of a statement by the great Philadelphia writer/performance artist/painter Homer Jackson, who has done a lot of work with young men in the prisons. The theory of a prison (or a penitentiary) is that the criminal will reconsider his life, and, by the time he's released, be ready to fit in. (The actual fact of American justice, however, is revenge and sadism, pure and simple. But more of that another time.) But the sad thing, Homer pointed out, is that these young men can't fit in. Not only have they come from a violent past and endured institutionalized violence, but the very notion of the normal is a fantasy perpetrated by the powerful. Language is among the fundamental agents in determining class status. So are race, dress, table manners, gesture, you name it.

Yes, poets have a place in easing these divisions, because cultural products can pass through social borders. My point in our conversation has been that poets must accept a contributing role. Changing language does not change society. The function of the "safe haven," be it the university, the political party, the church, even the organized hate group, is to establish exclusive modes of normality including language. Within any enclave, no prejudice exists. The difference between those who struggle and those who are comfortable is that the bitches, the coloreds, the cripples, the fags can never escape ridicule.

Poetry can be a powerful tool in questioning these conditions, but it is rarely given a chance. But it is beautiful and honest, and as much a part of the body as singing is.

KG: Poetry as part of the body — can you talk more about how exactly this works for you? And also, is poetry, for you, the same as singing? I know chant and song have played a huge part in your work — you spontaneously sing during readings and poems that work well READ lyrically. What history has most informed your connection of music and poetry? Where did all this song come in for you? Why sing?

GO: I think of the body at rest as a body of water. It is an instrument, played by the wind. Perhaps it is a field, a landscape, a wood. It is, certainly, an ecology, whose "weather" is emotional and psychological. Its physical form introduces the possibility of articulation. In voice-reading a poem, all aspects of physical being come into play. The lungs, chest, throat, glottis, mouth cavity, even skull are vibrant, sound transmitters. Posture is essential, denoting attitude toward the audience and discipline. Gesture introduces dance, and entirely new possibilities of expression. These things are what Blake referred to when he said that the body is the measure of all things.

In dream, the body becomes a landscape. Internal events have direct psychological interpretation. I believe that no one has ever reported a dream. They exist below consciousness. What we do is attempt to articulate them after waking, and that articulation is the trace which reveals our relation to the world.

Zukofsky's dictum — "Lower limit speech, upper limit music" — still serves, though it has begun to feel a little rigid to me. Legend has it that song served as the mnemonic for orally-based myths. If this is the case, then it is even more clear that poetry/song are linked to dance. I sometimes feel that the object of performance is to exhaust the body, so that only meaning remains.

"The beautiful" is what I'm talking about here. You see, the poet has a lot of instruments at her command, and any or all are capable of generating resonance, be it sympathetic or antithetic. I am almost about to propose that meaning is only possible in the encounter with something new, a revelation or a challenge. The poetry that does not do these things, but which simply reinforces existing worldviews or emotional scripts, is fake.

KG: Can you talk about how it is that "only meaning remains" after "performance exhausts the body"? Does the body's weather (emotion and psychology, as you said) get in the way of, or produce, meaning-making? In the beginning of *The Whole Note* — "pea green and troughing, sounds like poetry." Sounds like poetry is the body slooping its way through the thickest human goop. The body can be a body of water played upon from outside, or a fog inside of fog, or a storm in a fog. I like this — and I wonder what poetry is troughing for.

What you say about "new" — reminds me of "troubling the wound to outlast me." Rather than scarring over into the latest conventional appearance or expression, one might express the place where something is missing, the wound, where one "can codify uncertainty ... Albeit inaccurately." Woundedness, for me, is the location of learning. Perhaps the place one can be most in touch with the unknown is at the moment of learning? Every lesson includes an injury. Is the body ultimately where cluelessness, or emptiness, comes from, and/or can be expressed?

And you find Zukofsky's limit rigid — can you go into more detail about this? There is an interesting thread in *The Whole Note* regarding abstractions — "the length of my stride cored for pulp, for the preservation of abstractions." This fits with the wound/injury thread for me in "measure to sap / sentences lacking, subject, predicate, equilibrium, a pace implies home, identity, mine determined / to undermine a diagram." Equations can become as illusory as anything else. Are the areas that become scarred-over, where convention gets in the way of poetry? Who is wounded — language or the user?

GO: I can respond directly to some of your comments. For the most part, your questions answer themselves. (And it pleases me that you have read *The Whole Note* so closely!)

In Zukofsky we have someone who is deeply rooted in the classics and philosophy (particularly Spinoza (of whom I admit knowing little)), whose poetical statements and experiments pointed outward as radical tangents. Olson, too, is a poet like this (unlike, say, Pound or Laura (Riding) Jackson, who remained in the classical house, rebuilt it, but did not leave). As useful as Z's mathematical suggestion may be, it is a mistake to regard it as a definition, more than a challenge. The juxtaposition of speech and song (or as Zukofsky has it in "A-12", story — eyes: thing thought / sound) is useful, but it is also as ambiguous as its materials. Meaning is elusive in all cases, and it is present. The difficulty with speech is we expect it to convey meaning, and it therefore gets in the way. My argument is that music is not the only way or goal, not even for a poet. The world, in all its forms, enlightens, and we are capable.

Chax Press and Handwritten Press would like to think the following individuals, whose contributions made the publication of this book possible.

Nathalie Anderson

Bruce Andrews

Charles Bernstein & Susan Bee

Joan & Henry Braun

David Bushnell

James Cory

Robert DeSantis

Gerry Givnish

Aaron Goldblatt & Laura Campbell

Eli Goldblatt

Lyn Hejinian

John & Carol Hunt

The Kelly Writers House

Kevin Killian

Teresa Leo

Jackson Mac Low

Dr. & Mrs. Alan Ott

Gil Ott

Bob Perelman & Francie Shaw

Helen Plone

Joan Retallack

Vincent Rinella, Jr.

Joe Ross

Kerry Sherin

Ron Silliman

Juliana Spahr

John & Jennifer Taggart

Nathaniel Tarn

Heather Thomas

Craig Watson

Eleanor Wilner